T0169538

ONE-ON-ONE 101

ONE
-ON-
ONE
101

The Art of Inspired & Effective
Individualized Instruction

ROBERT AHDOOT

New York

ONE-ON-ONE 101

The Art of Inspired & Effective Individualized Instruction

© 2016 Robert Ahdoot.

All rights reserved. No portion of this book may be reproduced, stored in a retrieval system, or transmitted in any form or by any means—electronic, mechanical, photocopy, recording, scanning, or other—except for brief quotations in critical reviews or articles, without the prior written permission of the publisher.

Published in New York, New York, by Morgan James Publishing. Morgan James and The Entrepreneurial Publisher are trademarks of Morgan James, LLC. www.MorganJamesPublishing.com

The Morgan James Speakers Group can bring authors to your live event. For more information or to book an event visit The Morgan James Speakers Group at www.TheMorganJamesSpeakersGroup.com.

A free eBook edition is available
with the purchase of this print book.

CLEARLY PRINT YOUR NAME ABOVE IN UPPER CASE

Instructions to claim your free eBook edition:
1. Download the BitLit app for Android or iOS
2. Write your name in **UPPER CASE** on the line
3. Use the BitLit app to submit a photo
4. Download your eBook to any device

ISBN 978-1-63047-616-8 paperback
ISBN 978-1-63047-617-5 eBook
Library of Congress Control Number:
2015905206

Cover Design by:
Rachel Lopez
www.r2cdesign.com

Interior Design by:
Bonnie Bushman
The Whole Caboodle Graphic Design

In an effort to support local communities and raise awareness and funds, Morgan James Publishing donates a percentage of all book sales for the life of each book to Habitat for Humanity Peninsula and Greater Williamsburg

Get involved today, visit
www.MorganJamesBuilds.com

Habitat for Humanity®
Peninsula and
Greater Williamsburg
Building Partner

To my R's.

I can hear you playing in the next room.

TABLE OF CONTENTS

Acknowledgements

I've always believed in the concept of "it takes a village" to create anything of deep meaning and value. This work would not be possible without the consummately supportive communities rallying around me over the years, the members of which I must thank individually.

To the leadership of de Toledo High School—what can I say except that you gave me my wings. Without the trust, faith, and sense of partnership you instilled within me, none of my dreams would leave the ground, and none of the amazing work Yay Math has been able to achieve would ever reach fruition. The school's platform imparts to the students the merits of leadership, social action, and acts of kindness for the betterment of the world. The best part is that these ideals are not empty slogans. As a school, you not only promote the merits of creating social change to your students, but you also believe in it so much that you green-light your *teachers* to do the same. That proves, unequivocally, that your words and hearts are aligned. Yay Math is and will always be a universally accessible instrument of educational and social change. You recognized that, and you gave me the opportunity and tools to manifest such a high vision into reality. Words can never express my gratitude for taking a chance on me with nothing to go on during those first years.

To the students of de Toledo who partner with me to create such groundbreaking content, yay YOU! You are my perfect collaborators, serving as the voices for millions of people worldwide. Our live interaction, based on such a close relationship we have, is what gives Yay Math its incomparable soul. I only hope that our work together can serve as an example for what the synergy between a great idea and passion can coalesce into. And to my life-long friends on "Team Faculty," every day you make coming to work feel like coming home. For more than a decade, I have not had that "punch a time card" feeling at my job, all thanks to you. Thank you to each of you who gives me wisdom, guidance, support, and most of all *friendship* over the years: Bruce, Ellen, Gregg, Beverley, Jaimi, Howard, Matt, Becca, Alicia, Adina, Merzak, Etan, Sina, Mark, Yonatan, Kathi, Devin, Barbara, Michelle, Iris, Darren, Suzy, Dina, Jill, Sivan, Raquel, Cammie, Tami, Bobby, Stuart, Prudence, Earl, Orit, Gabe, Roger, J.B., Tammy, Diane, Shadi, Omer, Renée, Christine, Jess, Melanie, Tsafi, Joyce, Jared, Ray, and Tony.

To the viewers of Yay Math—can we say it one time together, "YAY MATH!" What a journey it has been together over the years. Yay Math is the vehicle that drives our worlds together, giving me the chance to learn about who you are—your struggles, your triumphs, and your dreams. As a whole, the reflection of humanity that I have had the chance to see through the Yay Math lens fills me with hope and invigoration about our world. I've met people who take the same standardized test five times in the hopes of getting past it to embark on their destined careers. I've seen students go back to school after twenty years away to manifest their goal of getting their degree. I've come into contact with students and parents of all ages, who rise to the occasion and succeed amidst a series of roadblocks found in and out of school. Just know that ALL my work is in service to you and people like you. You honor me with the level at which you pursue your dreams, and I am overwhelmingly proud to be in your corner.

Speaking of honors, what a huge one it has been to collaborate with my editor, Dr. Roberta Cheng Wolfson. I could not envision a better person for this huge task, both on a professional level as well as on a core identity level. Are you a fellow advocate for inspired education? Yes. Do you maintain an unwavering fidelity to clear, correct, and concise writing? Yes. Do you engage your work not as a mere job, but as a way of life, making your decisions based on morality and the advancement of our society? YES. If this book were a new schoolhouse, you would be its cement. Thank you from the bottom of my heart for your stellar work.

To the original Yay Math webmaster, Karen Eckstrom. You first used Yay Math to ace the math courses you needed to get your media arts degree. Then with your freshly minted degree, you personally reached out to me and offered to design, build, and maintain Yay Math's website purely as a gift of giving back. For years, you went above and beyond with your generosity, successfully delivering Yay Math's content to millions of people in a quality, fun, and easy-to-use way. Your family has become our family—our paths united always. Thank you for being Yay Math's champion from the beginning.

To my wife, Rinat. The word "support" pales in comparison to what you embody. Even from the days we starting dating and Yay Math videos were just beginning to take root, you'd watch them despite your admitted "Algebraversion." You've been there for me through every step of this journey, fueling me with inner peace. And given how education requires constant giving, having that sense of inner peace is the ideal headspace for me to do this critical work. When my classes and the world see me cracking jokes, performing like a nut, tuning into a class of confused students, high-fiving one elated student, or consoling another in tears, the love-energy behind all of that comes from you and our family. Suh my huh.

A Message From the Author

Tensions were high. The score was tight. The team was fighting for its life in single-elimination playoff basketball. The crowd screamed mercilessly in reaction to every move made by the players, coaches, and referees. Judging by the surrounding drama, the scene seemed suited for a world championship professional basketball game. This game, though, was only part of a fifth-grade recreational league, taking place on a Tuesday evening in a local community gym in suburban Los Angeles. I was the volunteer coach.

Those screaming members of the crowd were parents who had begun the evening in relatively stable form but had quickly spiraled into a frenzy as the game progressed. To be fair, the game was very intense. Yet all the while, as I looked out into the crowd of hysterical faces, or onto the court at the emotional expressions of all the players, I was awash in serene energy. I kept thinking to myself, "This is an elementary school recreational league. There are far more important things the kids will learn here than who will be tonight's victor." I made sure that the less talented members of our team got substantial playing time. During huddles, I saw the emotional looks on my players' faces. Some of the children were on the brink of tears even before the game was done. In addition to offering game-related strategy, I urged them to remember what this experience was all about: having fun, playing a game they loved, and working together as a team with strength and character. Afterwards, when we lost by a close margin, I told my sobbing group of boys how proud I was of them and how fortunate I was to be their coach.

At that point, I was a software engineer by profession. I had no background, training, or experience in teaching or education. Nevertheless, I felt comfortably in command of my role as a coach and mentor. The mom of one of my less talented players was so moved by her son's sense of belonging on the team that she insisted I meet her brother, the athletic director of a recently opened high school. I met him, got a job coaching the school's junior varsity team, and soon after was offered a chance to teach math despite my lack of experience. Many times when people start new employment, they say that they "found a job." I, on the other hand, believe that *my job found me*. I had finally discovered my true personal and professional calling in education.

When I first started out, friends and colleagues at the school called me "a fish in water" with the students. We "clicked," understood and respected each other, and harmoniously worked to achieve our mutual goals in the classroom. As the years progressed, the positive energy generated between the students and me grew to insuppressible levels. We knew that we had stumbled onto a classroom magic that was one-of-a-kind, and we adopted a conviction that other students would certainly benefit from such a fun, warm, and transcendent learning environment. One day, in the hopes of sharing our experience with others, my students and I perched a camcorder on top of a haphazard stack of books on a desk in my classroom, hit "record," and let the Yay Math movement come to life.

Yay Math (yaymath.org) is the premier source for free and openly accessible math video lessons, filmed *live* in my classroom. Often when teaching a filmed class, I dress up in costumes that have given life to now iconic online math characters, such as the "Mathemagician" and the "Mathemagyptian." Since its inception in 2008, Yay Math videos have come to be ranked number one through five on organic YouTube search results. Yay Math content is viewed more than two million minutes *per month* by people of all backgrounds in 180 countries worldwide. Yay Math's resonance with students has provided me the opportunity to give TEDx talks, to speak at schools about how to achieve inspired education, to blog for prominent education journals, and now to write this book.

Education has been my life for more than a decade now, but in hindsight, I realize that it has always been in the works for me, even from when I was a child. I have always had a knack for smoothly imparting ideas to people, for instantly ascertaining whether they understand or do not, and for spotting hidden fears or anxieties they experience during learning. I feel privileged to say that this is my gift, which I have committed my life to offering others in the hopes that their lives may benefit. Becoming a classroom teacher, then the founder of Yay Math, and now the author of a book on how to teach with inspiration are all simply part of an inevitable progression for me. This work is my highest service calling, and education is the forum by which I yearn to make the most positive effect on the world.

The field of education inspires me, challenges me, and motivates me to improve with each passing year. Such a level of commitment has equipped me with a wealth of experiences and ideas, certified by Yay Math's success, as well as by a burgeoning One-on-One practice in my community and online worldwide. My unfiltered voice in these pages, corroborated by the latest pedagogical research, combine to make what I believe to be a complete guide to success in the vital, growing field of One-on-One instruction. My deep hope is that this packaged wisdom offers you the tools to springboard to every height of personal success you have ever dreamed of.

My warmest regards,
Robert Ahdoot

Introduction

One-on-One is not just about tutoring. Is being a doctor just about medicine?

Doctors spend major chunks of their lives learning how to heal us. They go through fortunes of time, effort, and money to learn their craft. They toil through medical school, internships, residencies, fellowships, and then apply for positions in offices and hospitals worldwide.

And yet, after we make an initial visit to a new doctor, what do we say when someone asks us how it went? What are the primary topics of discussion when we speak about doctors? While we deeply yearn for doctors who went to the best schools and have every relevant certification, remarkably we don't begin our analysis of them with those "on-paper" descriptions. Rather, we first focus on whether they make eye contact with us, whether they answer all our questions, *how* they answer our questions, whether they smile and have a soothing presence, and any other qualities that reveal their level of *humanness*. We have even coined a term for it: "bedside manner," which is now firmly rooted in our lexicon. The personal connection we feel (or lack thereof) is paramount to us.

We surely appreciate the credentials on their walls; we may even coo over them. We would not be in the room with them in the first place had it not been for their credentials. Yet I believe that credentials must only be an implied starting point. We go to them saying, "I know you know this medicine stuff. I don't know this stuff. Please explain everything necessary to me, step-by-step, compassionately, so that I may heal." The starting point is the doctor's expertise. The end goal is our healing, fueled by a steadfast human connection with that person undertaking our care.

One-on-One education is no different. Doctors care for the wellbeing of our physical (and emotional/psychological) health. Educators care for the wellbeing of our academic (and emotional/psychological) health. Both are hired either to prevent or to address full-blown problems. Both fields deal in high stakes, ranging from the handling of long-term emotional wounds and feelings of despair, to the celebration of breakthroughs. For both doctors and educators, simply knowing the material alone does not guarantee their success. Many students have had at least one experience with a particular teacher who knew the stuff, but could not get it across.

That notion, of "getting it across," marks the impetus and burning need for this book. Let's explore the recent rise of the flipped and blended learning models. Flipped and blended learning entails students viewing educational content at home, and then spending time in school practicing those concepts with the aid of the teacher, who circulates around the room. Sal Kahn's *Kahn Academy* is a flagship driver of this model, which explicitly touts the merits of the One-on-One model over the One-on-Many. My question is this: assuming a teacher successfully flips her classroom environment, and at long last finds herself sitting across from her student… now what? Just talk about math, or science? Even before the proliferation of the flipped model, a huge part of the educational system has always relied on successful One-on-One exchanges. And now, adding up all the traditional schools, flipped classes, homeschooling programs, after school programs, One-on-One academies, independent study schools, and the ocean of extra help organizations out there, the need to define successful One-on-One practice is monumental.

Too many people incorrectly assume that almost anyone can communicate educational concepts clearly, if only they have expertise. What about the educator's cadence, body language, where she sits relative to her student, use of silence, use of praise, relatability, connectability, bilateral expectations, nonverbal tactics, golden phrases she can utter, breaking down walls, and the poisonous practices to avoid at all costs? We cover all that and so much more within these pages.

At long last, this book shines light on every strategy possible to transform an average One-on-One relationship into an inspiring one. This book is dedicated to every parent, educator, tutor, coach, colleague, boss, friend, and family member who wishes to communicate as an effective One-on-One artist, a term that I will define shortly. My mission is for us to celebrate and magnetize those synergetic moments when true learning happens, and then teach you to create those moments yourself. Fleeting yet unmistakable, these magical learning windows are the direct portals towards the collective advancement and enlightenment of our civilization. This is how I see education, and why it is my life's calling.

This book is primarily "how" oriented. In relatable terms, I will outline everything you'll need to know and do to become a master One-on-One artist. This book is also "who" oriented. This means that in addition to describing in detail *how* to do this sacred work, I will also build up to the idea of *who* you need to be for it.

Before we dive in, let's first create some common understandings. *The word "tutor" does not define this complex role. Therefore instead, I will use "One-on-One artist" or some variation.* There is nothing wrong with the word "tutor" itself; indeed, I tutor all the time. However, by acknowledging all the nuance and skill that goes into this role, this book is designed to forever turn you into successful One-on-One masters. The work reaches far beyond the transference of information from one person to another. It is about making connections in highly effective, creative, and inspiring ways to students who may be turned off, amidst a sea of peripheral challenges. It is about the deeply rooted understanding that we all learn best when we feel connected, both to the person delivering the information, as well as to the information itself. This book will completely cover how to establish that.

One-on-One symbolizes a level playing field, where teaching and learning occur in harmonious balance. Think of a typical one-on-one basketball game—both people are equally necessary and important, and no player is inherently superior over the other. Skill levels vary, of course. However, within the true spirit of the game, there never exists an imbalance of *power*. Both parties are equally powerful. In fact, even the capitalization of One-on-One is intentional. It invokes the sanctity of each individual present.

Let's next create an understanding about the differences between teaching and tutoring. The traditional classroom model, which matches one instructor with tens or hundreds of students, is naturally prone to creating confusion. I have experienced the following dilemma firsthand as a classroom teacher. In a matter of seconds, I need to decide: do I teach to the lowest performers in order to ensure that no one is lost? Or do I teach to the top performers, in my attempt to strive for the highest level of learning possible? Or do I find a middle ground and teach towards the average, ensuring that some students understand, some are bored, and some are bewildered? Such is one of many teaching dilemmas that spawn the need for individualized instruction. Other factors that add to the growing need for effective One-on-One instruction are decreased attention capabilities associated with the younger generations, educational budgets being slashed and classroom sizes growing, and an emerging demand for the educational experience to be more personalized and meaningful to the learners.

As a society, we debate over whether or not to decrease class sizes. Those for decreasing class sizes argue that smaller class sizes allow for students to enjoy more personal attention from their teachers. The smaller the classes, many reason, the more teachers will be available for each student. Through this logic, One-on-One learning (done correctly) is the *most* efficient and effective learning system in the world. Naturally so, because we cannot further decrease the number of students when the number of students is one.

One-on-One is also the true original form of teaching, as it starts at the earliest stages of life, between parent and child. And compared to the traditional classroom models we know today, One-on-One apprenticeship has been around for much longer and boasts iconic evidence of historical effectiveness. Leonardo da Vinci was a direct disciple of Verrocchio, who is lesser known today but was a leading artist in Florence at the time. Joe Higgs mentored reggae superstar Bob Marley, and in turn, Marley mentored hip-hop superstar Wyclef Jean. Coaches Phil Jackson and Dean Smith empowered basketball phenomenon Michael Jordan to achieve transcendent heights, as Jordan repeatedly cites how his growth and triumphs are directly linked to their relationship.

While individualized teaching is the most primary and most *primal* form of learning, it is nevertheless fraught with challenges. First, the One-on-One artist must fully immerse with the student. There is no podium to hide behind. There are no One-on-Many dynamics, which come with a higher level of anonymity and the ability to generalize the material so that it speaks to no one person in particular, with only the *hope* that individuals present might understand. Take a moment to imagine the act of directly engaging a person in front of you. In any given interaction, you would know whether or not he is listening. You would know if he is tuned in. This level of engagement requires social and emotional forms of intelligence that extend far beyond the actual learning material at hand. Another challenge with One-on-One instruction is that it can be time consuming, impractical, and highly expensive. The time has come to open the floodgates and no longer accept the idea that effective One-on-One education is reserved for the select few who somehow magically "get it" and know what to do. The value of this book is that it shatters that particular bottleneck and empowers all who read it to swiftly and successfully partake in this life-changing form of education.

Indeed, any teacher can have a noteworthy One-on-One moment with a student at any time, either during class time or throughout the school day. But the scope of our definition must not be limited to scholastic or academic topics only. If you have ever helped someone figure out how to use a function on her cell phone, advised a work colleague to hone a skill he needed for the job, or taught a friend how to chop an onion, then for those brief moments, you were engaged in One-on-One artistry. Learning happens all around us, all the time. I warmly offer you a full range of solid and intuitive ideas that can help all of us learn and grow together.

Chapter 1

SAY HELLO
(THEN SAY GOODBYE)
TO YOUR HISTORY

W hen my father, a world-class engineer, repeatedly attempted to teach math to my sister, who was in seventh grade at the time, they would always get into heated arguments. I doubt that the math homework itself, staring neutrally back at them from the page, was the reason they would spiral into their squabbles. Their personal and shared histories explained why they bickered so much during study time. Normally they got along just fine. So why the stark difference when it came to working together?

Fast-forward to when I first sit down with a new student. I ask him in a positive tone, "So how are we doing in the class?" Immediately, I may see looks of shame or anxiety spilling off his face, or possibly a smile that could mean a million things, followed by mumbles of "fine" or "not so good." My reply solely addresses his reaction, which is framed within his history. I'll say, "Look, I know it can feel uncomfortable that I, your parents, your teacher, or anyone else constantly asks you about this class. If this is unpleasant for you in any way, I totally get it; I've been there myself. But when I ask you, it's because I'm here to be on your team and help you figure it all out. So I ask that you tell me exactly what's happening, so I can understand the full picture, see what you see, and support you during this time. We'll go through it together." We don't resume talking about the class or the material itself until that new dynamic is established and understood. Planting those initial seeds of trust by acknowledging any discomfort the student might have is essential to counteract what could be years of built-up bitterness. Bitterness stops learning cold.

Of course, many people would be able to answer, "How are we doing in the class?" without hesitation or difficulty. But when you initially start to work with someone, you may be dealing with a student who has struggled mightily up to this point. Chances are high that students will answer that question and many other information-seeking questions while locked in the prisons of their histories.

I ask simply, "How are we doing in the class?" But silently, through the skewed lens the student adopts about the world or about himself, he interprets the question as, "You're not doing well in the class, thus you're inadequate. As a result, I'm going to yell/nag/punish/beat you. I'll let my own past fears or ambitions insidiously dictate our interactions, and sure enough, my disappointment will eventually wash over you long after this conversation ends. Besides my giving you a hard time, you'll also take my question as another opportunity to be hard on *yourself.*" The original question, by itself, is solely meant to gather information. It simply asks for an update on the student's standing in the class. Yet how can anyone answer it properly if his past has taught him to construe it differently?

I have seen the gamut of responses to this very question. Here are some major ones to look for:

- Parents may repeatedly chime in to give the answers, even when the questions are intentionally directed to the student. Such a situation may reveal a long-standing history of that parent overly controlling the child and, by extension, shutting the child down.
- Students may over-compensate for the shame, anxiety, or anger of having to report bad news either by lying or by answering with poorly timed jokes.
- Another response is for the student to say "I don't know" to every question asked, revealing a history of deflection and of not owning his/her responsibilities.
- The most devious way that someone's history might rear its head is whenever the response bears a hidden message lurking *behind* the student's words. Hidden within the student's response is the silent cry of "I'm not good enough." Tune in for when your student

uses words such as "impossible, stupid, hate, sucks," and blanket words including "always" and "never." For example, "Mr. Smith's tests are always impossible" or "I never get this stuff" or "Math sucks." Quite often, the student subconsciously may be saying, "I suck" in quiet despair.

Deep and inspired learning will never take place when students must simultaneously grapple with the real (and imagined) tolls that their histories have taken on them. Thus, starting at the very beginning of a learning relationship, any time a student betrays signs of a damaged history, the One-on-One artist must address the moment head on. I'm not talking about psychotherapy. I'm talking about small, tangible steps you must take to demonstrate to the student that you are well aware that past dynamics may be at play. One of those steps is embedded right into the question, "How are *we* doing in the class?" which very intentionally uses the word "we." The choice to use this collective pronoun moves away from singling out the student as a separate entity, which the word "you" insinuates. The use of "we" fosters the makings of a *new* history of shared experiences, unburdened by the weight of the past. Remember, when people go through rough learning histories, a main outcome is their feeling of isolation. It's lonely not to succeed. So looking for opportunities to naturally build bridges goes a long way towards eradicating their isolation.

The virtue of building bridges during the learning process (specifically to mitigate feelings of isolation) is a fundamental necessity, and one that has been under-examined and underutilized for far too long. Those tasked with teaching can tend to charge headlong into the content itself, without pausing and tuning in to the student in order to reaffirm their budding alliance. Maintaining this level of mindfulness, amidst any detrimental history a student brings to the dynamic, must be universal in and out of academic learning spaces. This concept easily applies to the workplace environment, for example. Imagine the case of a new employee who needs to learn the company's computer system. When the trainer checks in and asks the new hire, "Are we ok with this part?" this question conveys a sense of alliance with the trainee. For the time being, "I" and "you" don't exist; there is only "we." This type of strategy instantly eases the nerves of the trainee, who may be feeling isolated or anxious about learning the system in a short amount of time, framed against the backdrop of the pressure that comes with trying to make a strong first impression.

Over the course of their lives, countless people have equated learning with fear. Your duty is to establish a sense of dual ownership over the task of learning. When you take on the responsibility of teaching someone, you must help shoulder his or her burden. This small action will reduce fear and thereby re-define learning within the *current* framework that you establish, rather than perpetuate a possibly counter-productive past dynamic. Fresh dynamics ignite new pathways to breakthroughs.

Recognizing history does not mean dismissing history. In fact, we should do just the opposite. We should rejoice in the uniqueness of each soul. Each person enters the scene with a distinctive set of experiences, which we all must honor. Working to understand what each person brings to the learning table is a revealing and liberating consciousness and one that must not be overlooked. Imagine the doctor discussing cancer treatment options while the patient fights back his tears. In an ideal situation, the doctor would stop speaking to acknowledge the emotional moment. But why should only tears or other overtly emotional displays be acknowledged and dealt with, rather than the infinite other emotional "tells" that we bear, particularly when it comes to students and their learning?

Here are some student "tells," or verbal and non-verbal cues, that quietly reveal blockages to learning that students have developed over various points in their past. Tune in for:

- Fidgeting
- Looks of nervousness
- Looks of checking out
- Irregular breathing
- Trembling
- Excessive yawning (another sign of checking out)
- Frequent sighing
- Talking out of turn (e.g. answering questions before they've been completely phrased)
- Jumpiness, erratic behavior or speech (e.g. restless responses of, "Yeah, sure, uh-huh, yeah, sure…")
- Inappropriate or poorly timed sarcasm
- Standoffishness or cheekiness
- Aloofness, detachment
- Excessive and unnecessary apologizing to make sure he beats you to the realization that he's wrong, again.

Better that he points it out first before you have any chance to "discover" that about him.

If the One-on-One artist cultivates an awareness of the learner's history, then the impact on learning markedly improves. That awareness will give the One-on-One artist the perfect *approach*, tailored to each student. For instance, to the student accustomed to engaging her world timidly, then humility and humor can help her relax and come out of her shell. To the student who is not used to taking responsibility, jointly creating a system of accountability parameters will offer him a new sense of purpose. For the student who deep down believes she's not good enough, discreetly searching for opportunities to point out what she's doing right will begin to turn the tide of confidence back in the right direction, without making her self-conscious. Understanding each person's unique, precious, and oftentimes difficult history of learning has hugely positive ramifications, not only for the task at hand, but also for turning the page on all that holds us back.

Chapter 2

CREATING SPACES

T his book is about One-on-One mastery. In order to master this art form, it is vital to understand one underlying truth: a One-on-One master is measured more by who s/he is than what s/he does. This concept applies to every action in our pedagogical practice. In the words of Parker Palmer, author of *The Courage to Teach*, "[G]ood teaching cannot be reduced to technique; good teaching comes from the identity and integrity of the teacher." I completely agree with this higher form of assessment. Skills matter, but skills are not where the intangible magic lies. I will discuss this phenomenon more in depth in our last chapters.

The deeply interpersonal nature of the One-on-One craft requires a discussion about creating the right spaces. To understand what space means, let's first understand what "the absence of space" means. I deeply believe that the original goals and processes of learning have been hijacked by modern education. As a society, we are obsessed with what we can *measure*. Was the homework done, was the test grade good, and was the course passed? Did you at least turn in something to the teacher, even if it was sub-standard work? Students are admonished that they must at least turn in something, with the goal of getting some partial credit, rather than no credit. But in the professional world, turning in sub-standard work, simply because the deadline is at hand, would be highly problematic. Space provides us the opportunity to see the big picture behind our learning, and behind everything we do. Therefore we need that chance, or space, to understand how we work best and how to constructively improve.

Take, for example, one of my most despised educational phrases: Did that academic program "accept" you? The undertone connotations of the word "accept" are so detrimental to the psyche. On the one hand, since kindergarten we have been taught to accept people for who they are. On the other hand, we've created massively hierarchical systems (i.e. education, employment, social scenes), which deem us "in or out." It's ok not to accept certain behaviors, like disrespectfulness. It's ok not to accept the Discover card. It's *not* ok not to accept people. People have a fundamental right to grow safely as learners, at their own rhythm, so we must provide them with the room to do so.

When space is absent in our lives, we feel constricted. Palmer, in his earlier book, *To Know as We Are Known*, brilliantly describes the construction of space, as we know it. He contends that we certainly know the feeling of standing in a crowded bus versus standing in an open field. Or interpersonally, we know the feeling of friends or family members who constrict us with expectations or judgments, as opposed to those who offer us free reign to simply exist.

The mind works in similar ways. It knows when there is space to move around and mentally explore, and it also knows when its functions are being confined. In the introduction, I discussed our goal of opening "windows into the mind." Since everyone has unique learning styles and requirements, One-on-One artists must address and eliminate what could potentially be devastating blockages to creating sacred learning spaces.

On my second visit to a family's home to work with a student, I began the session by discussing his organizational habits. I asked to see his backpack. Soon enough, I realized that it was less of a bag and more of a jungle zone after a violent storm. Debris of teenage life abounded, items were entangled against others, and numerous documents wedged in notebooks aggressively stood guard against anyone who attempted to make sense of what was happening in there. I saw that it was time to let the space creation begin!

I asked him to bring a stapler, a hole-puncher, dividers, binders, and most importantly, a trash can. I was somewhat assertive too, which is generally well received by those who are perpetually disorganized and who are also ready to receive guidance in order to improve. It was as if we stood at the edge of that jungle together, machetes in hand. He appreciated having a non-judgmental partner to help him hack through it all. He and I would take out a handful of papers, and one-by-one, I would ask him, "Is this necessary or can we toss it?" And again I would ask the same question for each paper, and ask again, paper by paper. Soon enough, the process shortened to my asking, with some energetic gusto, "Keep or toss?"

This exercise was designed to show him that the decision to "keep or toss" was always his. I created the space *for him* to determine if each paper was a keeper or a tosser. With him making the decisions, I constantly helped him along his journey. For example, I prompted him with questions such as, "Do you need this for any future tests? Does the teacher expect you to keep something like this? Will you need this later?" If he said it was out, I *trusted him* to make that call, and out it went.

We threw out so much, much to the silent glee of mom, whom I spotted smiling at the other end of the kitchen. We even threw out empty paper lunch bags and gum wrappers. The jungle re-emerged as a backpack again. With all that extra room, we then put in a few pencils, pens, and his calculator in pockets of his choice. Then came the dividers. Anything deemed a keeper was hole-punched and placed in the correct section in the binder. For this reason, I always hole-punch anything I give my students. Without holes, one document leads to five, which leads to ten, which get shoved into pockets or slid into folders aimlessly.

To the average person, the sight of all that clutter actually *deters* her from even beginning any actual work. Feelings of being overwhelmed then lead to anxiety. At best, the student tries to work up the courage to get organized and may even tame her disorganized jungle on her own. At worst, she'll procrastinate until the point of shut down and simply end up staying away from the jungle in order not to face the chaos. Understandably so, the mess not only creates physical discomfort, but also elicits emotional discomfort too. The mess could be embarrassing, or provoke anxiety, or be another source of tension within the student's mind or among family members. The same goes with a disaster-zone garage, attic, or car trunk. Simply thinking about those zones, let alone correcting them head-on, can be a harrowing task that leads to inner and outer conflicts. This type of tension, born from the constriction of open space, shatters the learning process.

As the One-on-One artist, directly addressing messiness and supporting your student in adopting organized habits is a fundamental life skill you can offer. The same ideology applies to the actual workspace—is it clean and orderly? Is it quiet, well lit, and set at a comfortable temperature? Is it away from distracting dialogue by others in the vicinity, TVs, or other potential disruptions by pets, phones, gadgets, or children? Does it have an inviting, warm energy? To my core, I believe in the timeless act of creating warm, welcoming learning environments for students. These environments need to afford them the chance to have *unbroken* trains of thought, where they can allocate every potential ounce of brainpower they possess to immerse themselves in the task at hand.

Within reason, I'm all for using tools like music for certain subjects (such as art or math) to make the learning experience as pleasant as possible. And I acknowledge that some artistic souls thrive in chaotic environments. But overall, in our hyper-connected technological world rife with interruptions from text messages, emails, and social media, it is imperative that we give our students the chance to work in lengthier intervals of deep thought. The consequences are otherwise dire. The American Academy of Pediatrics has gone on record saying that a link exists between children's extended screen time and the rise of attention issues for children in school. Finally, the connection between too much tech and attention issues is not just heresay anymore; it's a researched fact. And all the while, my educator colleagues and I felt it to be true. Concurrent with the increasing prevalence of technology made available to younger and younger children, my colleagues and I have witnessed the evolving diminishment of attention capabilities in our students over each passing school year. Carving out space for students is a very real necessity to save them from themselves.

Creating physical and environmental space frees up a student's mind to imagine and discover. I have seen firsthand how minds work best when they operate in clean, open, generally quiet, and well-lit environments. It is our *obligation* to allocate such a physical space for our students, and in turn, teach them methods to maintain that valuable atmosphere.

Equally important to physical space is the *symbolic* nature of space. Do you know the type of people we could describe as "invaders?" They'll ask you a question only to tell you what they think. They'll talk over your statements. They won't wait for you to think before you respond; instead they will just inject their own take on the matter. And if your words contradict their beliefs, they'll make sure you know it. Just thinking about them makes me want to extend my palms outwards in a pushing-away motion, to mentally free up some space around me.

Now imagine that such invaders are parents, teachers, coaches, siblings, managers, supervisors, CEOs, politicians, colleagues, or friends. Each moment offers a chance for us to discover something new, but how can we discover anything amidst people who impose upon us? This imposition from invaders comes from what they say, do, and really what they represent—an invasive value system and how that makes us feel, even when they say nothing. To those of us who are very sensitive, like me, this type of energy eradicates any space for the mind and human spirit to produce original thoughts, to make mistakes in safety, and to elevate the plane of learning abilities. Tune in. Dedicate yourself to the creation and protection of space in all its forms, and not only will learning flow, but also you as the One-on-One catalyst will become a figure of stability and peace in your student's eyes.

Chapter 3

BYE-BYE, BOOK!

W hen it comes to technical subjects such as math and science, I wonder if textbook authors are aware of the staggeringly high and growing number of students who simply do not read the content within their textbooks. Here is a list of just a few subjects whose textbooks send students running for their lives: Algebra (in all forms, from elementary school to college), Geometry, Calculus, Statistics, Physics, and Chemistry. For generations, students have lugged around these textual bricks to reference them only during homework time. That is, they carry around the entire book just to do one exercise set a night, for example: "Page 235, #11–39 odd." Indeed, how odd it is.

Many teachers have become aware of the growing disenchantment with textbooks, so they use handouts and workbooks instead, which is a step in the right direction. But handouts and the like are less often a teaching tool and more often a practicing tool. While the brevity of handouts make them more tolerable to students, any document that is lengthier than a handout eventually sours them. Why the staunch reluctance to read through all that text, figures, formulas?

Think about the major skills and abilities you have learned through the course of your life. Let's discuss the timeless example of learning how to ride a bike. Before you started, did you look at a chart that described how the rotation of the bike's chain is powered by your pedaling? Did you read page after page, in sheer delight, about how squeezing the hand brake's air pressure system slowed the tires, about the pulley system of the bike's multiple gears, formulas on its torque or turning radius, or about how the bike's tire size and thickness relate to its speed and handle? No, that would be such a bummer! You just got on and figured it out.

You spent time getting a "feel" for the bike. You put on training wheels and after a little pedaling, you understood how you were more stable in motion than you were when still. Imagine the futility of explaining the concept of stability-in-motion to a child who has never ridden a bike before. Or better yet, imagine first introducing the concept of stability-in-motion to an adult by referencing pertinent physics formulas from a textbook. You would get nothing but blank stares. That's because optimal learning comes from *doing*. This process of *doing* applies to many relevant examples, such as learning how to work with technology or learning processes at the workplace. More and more frequently, especially with younger generations, people brush aside user manuals for any electronic device that comes in a box. They simply turn the gizmo on and begin to tinker with it.

The One-on-One artist has the following obligations: to support, explain as new questions arise, and be there to hold the backseat while the *rider* of the bike pedals. This philosophy applies not only to learning how to ride a bike, but also to learning how to do just about anything. The fundamental rule is that the learner must be the doer. Children are born preprogrammed with an innate curiosity to *do*. They pick objects up, fiddle with them, toss them aside, and repeat the process for almost everything they encounter. Then later in life (at our jobs, for example) we return to that same realization— that the ideal way to learn is through undertaking processes ourselves, compared with solely being shown how. However, in between our young childhood and adulthood years, during the schooling period of our lives, we are compelled to deviate from the "learn-by-doing" principle. In traditional school settings, learning becomes passive, based more on a philosophy of "teach me how, while I sit back."

Bear in mind that "teach me how" is not necessarily the wrong approach. Students need clear and concise instruction, both for the technical courses listed previously, as well as for other complex disciplines such as writing, reading comprehension, the arts, and foreign languages. Their aversion to reading textbooks is at the heart of their dire need for quality instruction. And yet, schools still expect the student to learn through reading those texts. Such a practice has been ironclad protocol, at all levels, for generations. But generations change. Thrown into the mix now is a growing population of entrepreneurial students always on the go, home-schooled students, students engaged in independent study, students returning to school after many years, and students viewing content online using a video-based approach, including online courses and flipped learning. Add all these people up and you've created an astounding population of time-strapped, textbook-opposed students who are otherwise well-intentioned learners.

How can we counteract book aversion? One antidote is to start at square one, and since the pun beckons, starting at square one renders us "Square One-on-One artists." The Square One-on-One artist taps into the eagerness and hope we all experience when we know that we can start our journey at the beginning. Armed with this knowledge, learners feel immensely relieved. When people are taught concepts in increments, starting with blank paper or clean boards, using layered scaffolding, the information becomes digestible. On the other hand, trying to absorb a finished product in the form of a technical book with already completed diagrams and tables is far more intimidating.

Here is my call to action for any topic that is taught from a book or manual. One-on-One artists are at our best with the basics: pencils, pens, blank paper, blank computer screens, clean boards, our voices, ears, eyes, and hands. These are our brushes and canvases. Teaching someone math? Start with a simple, introductory problem on blank paper and observe how easy/difficult it is for the student to do. Teaching someone how to read music? Start with the simplest of notes and keys. Even during follow-up lessons, synchronizing from square one is an invigorating reminder to the student of how far he has come, as well as an indicator of exactly where he needs to resume study.

Below, I provide a template for effective "Square One-on-One" instruction. My template is a more detailed dive into the "Gradual Release of Responsibility" (GRR) model offered by Doug Fisher and Nancy Frey. In the GRR model, the educator's approach traverses from "I do it" to "We do it" and eventually to "You do it." Let's explore this trajectory within the One-on-One framework.

At the outset of learning new material, virtually all the information resides within the educator. That educator initially shoulders the responsibility to transfer the information during the early stages. As the learner demonstrates more understanding and makes progress, she takes on more of the learning onus, to a point when teacher and student are working in unison. Eventually, the student reaches a stage in which she knows enough to claim full ownership of the tasks and exhibits proficiency without assistance. In the template below, I chronologically break down every energetic exchange within this release of responsibility flow, in which I am the instructor and you are the student. Following each exchange is sample dialogue on the algebraic topic of simplifying square roots. The dialogue serves to contextualize the goals of that particular exchange in greater detail.

Exchange #1

I explain / I show how
You observe

I begin at square one, "So, when thinking about square roots, we need to begin by understanding what a 'perfect square' is. A perfect square is the result of multiplying a number times itself."

Exchange #2

I explain / I show how / I check in (i.e. by asking, "So far, so good?")
You observe / you ask anything

I continue, "Let's go through those perfect squares. 1 times 1 is 1, then 2 times 2 is 4, and 3 times 3 is 9. So far, so good?"

You ask, "Ok so perfect squares are 1, 4, 9, then... 16... 25, 36, and so on?"

I answer: "Correct."

The learning onus already shows signs of shifting onto you.

Exchange #3

I explain / I show how / I check in
You observe / you ask / you try

I continue, "Now let's see if we can find perfect squares 'hiding inside' other numbers, which are called 'factors.' Meaning, we know that 12 is not a perfect square, but 4 is, which is a factor of 12, because 4 times 3 is 12. Make sense? Can you try one, let's say, 18? Is 18 a perfect square? If not, can you find any perfect squares 'hiding inside' the number 18?"

You respond, "Well 18 is *not* a perfect square because there is no number times itself which is 18. So I have to look 'inside' 18 for numbers that can multiply to make 18 that *are* perfect squares. Oh—9 and 2—because 9 is a perfect square."

Exchange #4

I explain / I show how / I check in
You observe / you ask / you try / you do

I say, "That's right. So let's go back to 12. You said 4 and 3 multiply to 12. Now all we need to do is take the square root of both those numbers, first 4, then 3. The square root of 4 is…"

"2."

"Yes, and multiply that by the square root of 3. So what's the answer to the square root of 12?"

"2 times the square root of 3. So this process will work with any number?"

"Yes. Try the square root of 18 again."

You say, "Since we figured out that 18 is not a perfect square, we found perfect squares that multiply to make 18. We said they are 9 and 2. Now I take the square root of both those numbers. The square root of 9 is 3. The square root of 2 remains just that. So the answer is 3 times the square root of 2."

Exchange #5

I show more
You do / you do more / you ask

I go on, "Indeed you want to find the perfect squares hiding inside, but you really want the *biggest* perfect square hiding inside. Try the square root of 32, for example."

"Well, 32 isn't a perfect square, so what about 4 times 8?"

I remind, "Yes, 4 times 8 is 32. But remember, you want the *biggest* number hiding inside 32 that is *still* a perfect square."

You think for a moment before offering, "Ok I see! 16 times 2? I take the square root of both 16 and 2; so the answer is 4 times the square root of 2?"

Exchange #6

I answer

You do / you do more / you check in (i.e. by asking "Is this the idea?")

"Yes. Try the square root of 300."

"Ok, well I was thinking 25 times something makes 300, but an even bigger perfect square than 25 is 100. So if 100 times 3 is 300, and I take the square root of 100 times the square root of 3, then I'm left with 10 times the square root of 3. Do I have the idea?"

Notice how much less I speak in these final exchanges.

Exchange #7

I challenge

You do / you do more / you show how

"Yes, bravo. The key is finding that largest perfect square hiding inside, which we call a factor. Talk to me about the square root of 108."

You reply, "I'm tempted to try 4, but I feel like there's a bigger number hiding inside..." Then you proceed to take the reigns and show me how to figure out the problem.

Notice that within the seven exchanges, the complexity increased *in tandem* with the responsibility shifting onto the learner. In other words, once your student speaks your language, he can incrementally take on very complicated information, without him necessarily realizing how far he's come. The image that comes to mind is that of a tennis instructor. The instructor's main job is to present the perfect lobs for the player to swing at, based on player skill. Naturally, those lobs may begin as very gentle. Perhaps several lobs in a row will be markedly similar, for the player to gain some confidence and momentum. But as the player advances, the instructor's lobs become swifter and less predictable. The player is now so immersed in her zone that she is unaware of far she has come. The instructor masterfully built up the intensity in such a way to keep the student fully engaged in the moment. We must apply this same notion of square-one build-up to our One-on-One practice, in order to diffuse student book aversion. The over-arching problem with books is that they fail to scaffold with such acute human awareness. That failure is the primary source of book aversion.

Let me be clear in saying that we absolutely need books to encapsulate all the information associated with a given topic. Books are often used as references. We consult them when we need information, images, diagrams, examples, and so forth. However, we must be the masters and make books our servants, not the other way around. For this reason, I strongly advocate using a non-book approach during the early and intermediate stages of learning, as part of the One-on-One method. Your mastery of the subject is critical for your students. YOU are their book. YOU are their reference, so be the intuitively elegant canvas they need you to be. Students can turn to books once they get going and learn enough so that they may teach themselves. That ultimately is the endgame—teaching learners how to learn. The road to getting there, though, is to first set the books aside and just deal with the information, human-to-human.

A friend of mine described a common scene from a recent trip to his home country that will forever play in my mind. Late Saturday night, several coffee shops situated side-by-side were teeming with young adult students. Each small, round, wooden table seated several people, many of whom were animatedly debating math and science formulas scrawled hurriedly on restaurant napkins. The din of intensive yet positive learning was pulsing in the air. This was quite an effective learning environment: highly socialized and simplified, with no power dynamics or academic pressure. And of course, no textbooks were in sight, only napkins. I like to imagine that the most groundbreaking ideas in history originated from notes scribbled on napkins, long before they were printed neatly in formal textbooks. We don't necessarily need hefty textbooks to initiate our learning, because real learning can indeed spark up anywhere, even on something as small as a coffee shop napkin.

Chapter 4

TO-DO'S

This chapter is dedicated to outlining concrete strategies for you to instantly implement. Some or all of these will work for you. They have taken me half my life to accumulate, and each is a uniquely essential system for us to increase student learning.

Synchronicity

One-on-One teaching is at its core a service position. Your role is to support, encourage, and uplift your students whenever naturally possible. But this must be done correctly. In tandem to your student's learning process, you must work to understand your student's perspective. Your goal is to paint a mental picture in your mind of what your student's life is like within his current learning situation. By tuning in and synchronizing your mind to your student's, you'll let your student know that he has found a trusted advisor in you. Offer healthy amounts of affirmation that you understand and see what he currently deals with. Keep in mind: you are there to offer him simple affirmation, not any dramatic sympathy. "Wow, dealing with a teacher so disorganized sounds stressful, I hear you," is affirmation. "Oh no! I'm sooooo sorry that you have to deal with that! Yuckypoodles for you" is sympathy run amok.

The One-on-One relationship is an intimate one. You are your students' mentor, advisor, coach, and, eventually, friend. You are *not* their therapist. When offering counsel borders on counseling, steer the conversation back to your domain and be ready to involve anyone you deem necessary for additional support, such as parents, counselors, or clergy.

Synchronicity is just that; it is the act of synchronizing yourself with your student, of taking a stroll in your student's shoes to experience life from his vantage point. This usually takes place at the beginning of meetings. Following such dialogue and after the meeting takes place, it is paramount to remember some of the main themes in his life. That way, you can follow up with him during future sessions, and advance the relationship's momentum.

Here are some synchronicity starters:

- What's it like in class? (This is a big question. Topics include teacher style, teacher value system, general classroom demeanor, grading policies, level of consistency or lack thereof, level of inspiration or lack thereof, etc.)

- What's the teacher like; how well do you connect with him/her?
- What other stuff do you have going on? (i.e. teams, clubs, work, commitments, etc.)
- How do you feel about having had to… ? (e.g. switch courses, take the SAT again)
- What's been your experience with… ? (e.g. subject matter, task at hand, etc.)
- Do you like doing this? (People really enjoy sharing how much they like/dislike the topic.)
- What are your goals? (described next)

On your mark, get set, GOAL

Surprisingly, when we begin working with people, we oftentimes fail to ask them what their exact goals are. Sometimes at the outset the goal is obvious, e.g. to achieve a certain score on the ACT. But sometimes, the goal is unclear. In academia, goals range from improved grades to improved confidence. Some students want an A, while others fight for a C, and still others just want to learn more. When the time is right, and with sensitivity, you may need to manage some of your student's expectations in order to avoid a setup for big disappointment. Don't torpedo your student's dreams, but point out to her if it is mathematically impossible to raise her D-level grade to an A before the end of the term. Then help her look ahead to performing strongly at the outset of the following term.

Each student's goal is a guiding sign that can help you tailor your sessions. Some students are very results-driven. If so, respect their mindset, synchronize with them, and work with them to create tangible milestones. Some students are less interested in results and more interested in simply learning and understanding better. Herein lies the underlying goal that all One-on-One artists need to strive for. Through our actions and conduct, *our fundamental goal is to elicit the students' interest in learning and to equip them to become avid lifelong learners.* Teaching a student how to solve problems or how to beat a test is where we begin. Instilling within them a sustainable intellectual curiosity is where we finish. The roadmap to achieving this outcome is outlined in chapter eight.

Seating arrangements

If your One-on-One session involves sitting down with the student and writing, first find out whether he is right- or left-handed. Then sit on the opposite side of his dominant hand, so that you can clearly see his writing. This small detail does wonders. Sitting next to his dominant hand does not work well, as it ensures that the writing hand blocks what is being written from your perspective. In order to see what's being written in real-time, you would need to crane your neck or peer over their hand, which can be invasive of the student's space. Sitting next to the student's dominant hand may also require you to wait for the writing to conclude and then for the paper to turn towards you for you to be able to see what was written, which done repeatedly is a waste of time and a break in flow.

The ideal seating layout would have you sitting perpendicular to the student, if possible—not next to and not across from the student. Sitting directly next to a student is not terrible, but it forces both of you to work harder to face each other during moments of dialogue. On the other hand, a true One-on-One master can actually sit across from the student, as long as he or she can easily read the student's writing from an inverted vantage point. Another key requirement of sitting across from the student is to be able to actually *write* upside down, a skill that I have diligently developed over the years, which happens to entertain my students. Again, your best position is next to the student's *non-dominant* hand, so that you have a clear line-of-sight of the dominant writing hand at all times.

Who's in control?

After synchronizing, and once short term and general goals have been established, the One-on-One practitioner sets the session on its course. We must have a general plan for how to get the student from square one to square one hundred and work in partnership to steer her towards that result. However, the student has a hand on the steering wheel too. Submit to the fluidity of each moment. If the student suddenly poses tangentially relevant questions, for instance, this is a very good sign. It reveals her blossoming intellectual curiosity we so critically need to foster. In fact, seize those moments to ask additional related questions on top of her questions. Keep a light grip on the reigns. Of course, bring the session back on course if there is no end to the sidebar in sight, or if you are getting too far off topic. But within reason, allow (and encourage) your student's overtures of ownership.

Any discussion about control necessitates a discussion about the *perception* of control. Let's explore the difference between two similar One-on-One offers:

"Let me show you how."

"May I show you how?"

Chances are certain that both statements will lead to the "showing how." However, the first implies that the teacher is in control. The second implies that the *student* is in control. This is a potentially huge pivotal moment in the learning dynamic. Oftentimes if someone is in the throes of learning something unfamiliar and it isn't going well, he may feel an entire loss of control over his situation. He may also be confronting negative internal narratives based on his history, narratives such as, "Why can't I ever understand this?" or "This always happens." A loss of control, or even the *perception* of the loss of control, undermines the necessary levels of stability and confidence that people need in order to learn in their best form. Therefore, asking "May I show you?" implicitly offers control *back* to the student.

This choice of words is particularly effective, because it elegantly realigns the natural balance of power. Remember, pure One-on-One instruction must never consist of an authoritarian relationship. The One-on-One artist already possesses some authority within the learning dynamic, simply due to his expertise of the material. But proficiency does not entail superiority. Students tacitly pick up on the quiet confidence required for us to offer them a real stake in their learning process. They appreciate and respect it. Every now and then, subliminally offering some degree of control back to the learner sends a magnificent message: that teaching and learning are never about ego.

"Objection: Leading Question"

The following strategy is very nuanced and must be timed and implemented appropriately. And when done correctly, it's highly effective. Suppose you are teaching a student a certain process. You ask a series of questions, each of which begins with "How do you...?" Hopefully the student knows how to answer them. As your student progresses to a higher level of understanding, try asking a "How do you...?" question for something which *cannot* be done. For example,

"How would you draw a circle with radius equal to negative 3?"

Student chews on the question for a while. Then he offers, "But how can you draw a negative radius?"

"Exactly."

"So it can't be done then?"

"Correct. Therefore what's one rule regarding the radius, always?"

"The radius has to be positive."

"Indeed, like my mood right now."

See how much more effective this approach is compared to merely asking, "Can a circle have a negative radius?" Asking *whether* the circle can have a negative radius invites the possibility that it can or cannot, making the question leading in nature. Leading questions are easier to answer, naturally, as embedded within them are clearly marked avenues to the answers. Thus One-on-One practitioners can leverage leading questions to help novices get warmed up to certain topics. Down the line, though, occasionally using non-leading, incorrect questions is a wonderful way to challenge the students to think on their own. It keeps them on their toes, ready to question everything you say, which is an excellent tactic to mold them into capable citizens. We want to foster within our students the innate inclination to think critically, and to do so, they must *question* critically. Students who can "question our questions" are on the fast track to advancement.

Some more examples of falsely leading questions are:

1. "What's the square root of −81?" (Answer: There is no real square root of anything negative.)

2. "How would you demonstrate an example of a colon fixing comma splice?" (Answer: Colons do not resolve comma slice, but commas paired with coordinating conjunctions do. They are FANBOYS: for, and, not, but, or, yet, so.) Semicolons fix comma splice as well.

3. "Suppose I drop a ball from the top of a ledge. Assuming I know how fast it accelerates to the ground, how hard will it hit the ground?" (Answer: Missing information. We would either need to know how high the ledge is, or how much time the ball fell.)

Explain to your students that once they show signs of advancement, you may sometimes ask incorrect or non-leading questions. It will compel them to listen to you with a more critical ear and will prime them for heightened independent thinking.

"Are you sure?"

In the globally popular television game show, "Who Wants to be a Millionaire?" contestants answer trivia questions which can eventually win them lots of money. Arguably, the most climactic part of the show is when the host asks the contestant, "Is that your final answer?" By design, that question always heightens the drama. It is the *finality* of the answer that makes people so uncomfortable. Why is that?

Undoubtedly, we have a deep-seated fear of being wrong. Saying that our answer is final leaves no backdoor to escape from if we are incorrect. That is why many students, of all ages, answer questions with some trepidation. They may answer a question in the tone or form of another question, e.g. "Is the answer B?" Or, they may add qualifiers to their answer, to lessen their commitment to their statement, in case they need to immediately back off whenever wrong, e.g. "I <u>think</u> the answer could <u>maybe</u>/<u>possibly</u>/<u>probably</u> be B, <u>perhaps</u>." Let's explore this phenomenon further.

At some point in our increasingly insecure culture, we came to associate the question, "Are you sure?" with the statement, "You may be wrong." At face value, the words "are you sure?" combine to form a neutral question: whether or not you are certain about what you have just said. At its core, this is an unbiased question. But through the filter of our life experiences and history, we have come to hear many underlying messages beneath this question. Maybe our parents asked us, "Are you sure?" when they wanted to subtly steer us in another direction. Or maybe we ask our friends/partners this question to let them know that we don't agree with whatever they have just said. Either way, your involvement is huge here. In partnership with your student, hit the "reset button" on this question, and return its meaning to its original neutrality. Challenge your student to stand by his answers with improved conviction.

Try this experiment: ask a student if he is sure, even when he is correct. Better yet, ask him *especially* when he is correct. Remove all tone from your voice when asking. The question is not a game or a chance to be cute; it is purely a business question. Your student's response will reveal huge data on how he handles himself. This data you will then use to build your student's *confidence*, from the ground up. Suppose you ask your student for an answer to a certain question. He replies,

"I think then that the answer is 10."

You ask in a neutral tone, "Are you sure?"

He pauses. "Is it not 10?"

"I didn't say that, I'm just asking if you're sure about your answer."

He pauses again, checks over his work, and maybe talks through it aloud, looking to you for facial/verbal cues that he's on the right track. You do him a favor by remaining neutral through his process. "Yeah, 10, I think so," he says somewhat timidly.

"Ok, so why do still sound unsure?"

"I don't know, I guess you thought I was wrong."

Here's your chance to build confidence. "Just because I ask you if you're sure doesn't mean you're wrong. I'm just asking if you're sure. So are you sure it's 10?"

"Yes."

"Very nice, yes, the answer is 10." OR "Ok, you're almost there. You did everything right up to here..." Whether or not he's right is irrelevant; the goal is for the student to stand by his answer. Condition your student to bear no connotative relationship with the question, "Are you sure?" Simply use the question to examine his certainty.

In the preceding exchange, first notice how the student interprets the question. He immediately assumes that "Are you sure?" means that the answer is *not* 10. His immediate tendency to disavow his own answer illustrates the rampant "conviction deficit" embedded within so many realms of our lives, especially education. The instructor in the above exchange is slowly reprogramming the student's hardwired tendency to self-doubt. "I didn't say you were wrong, I just asked if you were sure," and "Just because I ask if you are sure doesn't mean you're wrong" are statements that fly in the face of what we have come to subscribe to as a society regarding the interpretations of "Are you sure?". This manner of reprogramming is an uphill climb, but the benefits hold life-changing promise.

Next, notice how during the student's checking process, the instructor does not give anything away that would rob the student of this opportunity to independently check over his own work. Will you be there for your students during their tests or during other high-pressure situations? Since we can't sidle up next to them during major exams, we owe them every chance to master the full spectrum of their responsibilities from beginning to end without any premature bailouts from us.

Finally, we see that "Are you sure?" works for both correct and incorrect student answers. The insights we gain from this One-on-One moment provide us a newfound ability to address any underlying insecurities in the student's problem-solving *process*. Being wrong is not a bad thing, in fact, just the opposite. Convey to your student that being wrong actually is a vital part of real learning. The question, "Are you sure?" solely seeks to ascertain the student's sense of conviction, and subsequently improve upon it. If young students grow to adults and never resolve the insecurities they may associate with problem-solving, then we will flood our population with thin-skinned conformists who will struggle to take a stand in their lives.

Jumbled bricks tumble walls

In their book, *Make it Stick: The Science of Successful Learning*, Peter Brown, Mark McDaniel, and Henry Roediger III cite a fascinating study involving the ability of eight-year-olds to master a task, in this case, tossing beanbags into buckets. Half the group practiced throwing bags into buckets that were three feet away, and the other half of the group practiced throwing bags into buckets that were two and four feet away. Following twelve weeks of practice during gym class, all students were tested on tossing bags into the three-feet-away bucket. Remarkably, the students who practiced on the two- and four-feet-away buckets were overwhelmingly more successful than the students who practiced on the three-feet-away buckets. This tells us that differentiation *matters*. The path to mastery is not linear. It meanders, touching on as many peripheral topics as reasonably possible. The beanbag experiment highlights this. One cannot be a master of throwing beanbags in a bucket only three feet away any more than a proficient bike rider can be a master of only riding downhill. Throwing bags, riding bikes, and all significant learning endeavors must be approached generally, to prepare the student for all upcoming circumstances.

One of the inherent values of starting from square one is our ability to mentally log where we cover various topics on the page. During your session, create an intuitive and segway-driven system in which each topic flows naturally into the next. But once your student understands a few concepts and you've moved on to newer territory, prime him to be ready for you to jump around to anything you've already covered, especially after some time has passed.

The best analogy that encapsulates this paradigm is laying brick. The bottom layers must come before higher layers. The process of laying each brick is a meticulous one, which involves carefully setting cement, making small corrective adjustments to the brick, and being ready to pull off the current brick to reset it anew if necessary. At any given moment, 100% of the builder's attention is focused on the individual brick at hand. However, once all of the bricks have been set and some time has passed for the cement to harden, the brick-layer can see that every single brick gains its strength and value from the many bricks all around it.

As One-on-One educators, we are builders too, but of minds, not bricks. Just as all builders do, we are *obligated* to check the foundation, regularly and without notice. Imagine the shock of jiggling free a low-level brick from the foundation of a building. That same shock must exist in education—not in the form of gasps or disappointment in our students—but rather more in the ironclad acknowledgement that jumbled bricks tumble walls.

Build each brick of knowledge upwards, slowly and carefully. Then over time, jump around to any peripherally related content to check for solid foundational understanding. If your sidebar tangentially leads you to areas that need more attention, either make a note to return, or push through it if necessary for the current task(s) at hand. Also explain to your student and/or parents how important it is to work on foundational or related material. If you were to uncover a live mine on the battlefield, the right thing to do would be to spend all the time necessary to defuse it, immediately. This is good practice both for the act of learning and for life in general.

Back to the future

The following tactic is solid gold, definitely one of my lifetime favorites. Suppose your student struggles to understand a concept. Then after piecing it together with your assistance, she experiences her much sought-after "aha!" moment. Precisely then, say the following, "Ok, Jess, it seems like you get it now. So could you please go back in time, let's say ten seconds, and explain to the Jessica of ten seconds ago what she didn't know then, but that you know now?" Students get a real kick out of thinking of multiple versions of themselves. They even may laugh a little while pretending to talk to themselves. Remember that your request is not rhetorical; insist that they do this exercise despite any discomfort at its newness or "weirdness."

Through your framing of this activity, students will implicitly comprehend how the "updated" versions of themselves regenerate in a matter of seconds. This fun time-travel thought experiment is a creative way to *make them aware of their own progress*. The notion that progress conceivably occurs within any ten-second interval encourages them.

Stepping back, we know how many younger students are consumed by receiving immediate feedback, as they are being brought up in a world saturated with technology and gaming. One of the chief reasons students gravitate towards technology and games is the immediate feedback those platforms provide. Swipe this, then see that. Tap this, then that happens, and so forth. I do not advise acquiescing to this sometimes-addictive need for constant feedback by frequently throwing it their way. In general, tacitly teach your student how to exist comfortably through longer intervals of less feedback, for the bigger rewards later. Those larger rewards may be test grades, semester grades, a job well done, or the natural satisfaction of overall understanding and achievement. In the next section and next chapter, I go into further detail about the crucial role that feedback plays in your practice. But in this particular case, your student worked to achieve her own "aha!" catharsis. Since her progress is self-produced, offer her a way for that progress to also be self-*realized*, through a conversation with "herself" of ten seconds ago. Have some fun with this one.

Baby got feedback

It is no overstatement: One-on-One education is an *art form*. You combine technical expertise with high socio-emotional intelligence to give your student a supreme learning experience. As such, art entails creativity. How you engage and offer your student feedback are major opportunities to add creativity to your craft. How often do we really think about the exact phrases we say during sessions, and about the precise impact they have? Below is a list of some common phrases, paired with *less* common phrases that deliver the same message but with some uplifting flair. We could use a common approach, but why settle for common when every minute is a chance to entertain and inspire?

Common phrase	Alternative way to say it	Examples and insights
That's right.	I couldn't have said it better myself.	
Want to try?	Want to drive?	The image of driving works well with teens.

You're doing well.	You're in the zone now.	The concept of "the zone" heightens the experience, such that the student feels as if he's performing on a theatrical stage or in sports.
This may help…	The good news is… (Framing a good learning tip as "good news" gives a positive spin on what you say, which students appreciate. After all, who doesn't love good news?)	e.g. "The good news is that this problem is just like the other one we did."
What do you expect to see on the test?	Pretend to be your teacher. What would she put on the test?	This strategy offers a higher degree of empowerment, because it makes the student *pro*actively prepare, rather than *re*actively respond.
Take this, for example.	Take your friend, for example. (Personifying a component of the assignment or question as your student's "friend" is unexpected and disarming, but in a delightful way.)	e.g. "Take your friend, the ribosome, for example."

| I know this is hard. | You're a warrior. | Once you say this, students feel compelled to live up to the honor of being a warrior. It's uncanny how well it works. |
| You got it! | You nailed it! / You're owning it! / Bang! / Look at you! / Wow! / Swag. / Chill. / Tight. / Word. / Dope. / Bingo! | These expressions come and go with the times. What's important is to find what's hip and try them out at key moments during your sessions. Even if a phrase flops, it's funny! |

These are just some examples that illustrate the potential for our words to carry uplifting power. Certainly, only speak words that align with your personality and style. Never be inauthentic, and remember to stay your core self, as students can spot discomfort and over-trying from miles away. Having said that, try splicing in colorful language to pique their interest. As their ambassador to the information, we confront what may be very dry material sometimes, so entertaining the student goes a long way towards keeping them engaged.

Try language tools such as hyperbole (e.g. "Solving this problem is your key to the Promised Land.") or personification (e.g. "Which of these will win the battle?") to breathe life into the content. Or perhaps, trying throwing in a line from a current hit song, TV show, or movie when your student would never see it coming. In order to become a One-on-One expert, you must recognize the intensive *performative* nature of this profession. We are performance artists, calling upon faculties of mind, body, and spirit for this type of work. Hypothetically, if you and your student are immersed in this art while sitting at Starbucks, and people at the nearby tables pause, listen in, and smile, then you may be doing something right.

"Why?"

One day as a seven-year-old, during a conversation with my uncle, I asked him "why?" about something that apparently intrigued me at the time. He answered. Then I asked "why?" again, to which he answered. According to him, I asked "why?" with relentless curiosity during that particular conversation. It seems that I just needed to hear "why" for every new piece of information presented to me.

Extend this courtesy to your student, hopefully with less childish insistence than my seven-year-old self. At regular intervals, ask her why a certain rule, theory, or answer exists. Notice that if she struggles to answer, then asking "why?" is exactly the right question. The "why?" question sometimes runs the risk of frustrating the student, because it can be among the most difficult questions for her to answer. Should you see this frustration bubbling up in her, explain to her that the ability to fully articulate the concepts in her own words, without assistance, is an integral part of mastering any topic. Feel free to walk her through the explanation, if you see her struggling with it at first. But never let her complete rote processes mindlessly, without a healthy amount of big picture awareness along the way. "Why?" reveals the fundamental truths *behind* those processes. Asking "why?" is so important that even if she stumbles on a single word within her answer, kindly ask her to recite the full answer again, to perfection. Remember the reason for asking why: jumbled bricks tumble walls.

Finally, asking "why?" lets your student know that your intention is to teach him on the deepest of levels. A student can tell if you are teaching on only a basic level, which generally entails a process-centered approach. Without any "why," the process comes across as meaningless, as in: first do this, then do that, then this, and repeat. But if we dig deeper and sincerely wish to coax the "why?" out of the student, then we reveal our high level of commitment to their meaningful learning. This question shows that you care and that you are thorough.

"Yes-anding" and "I know what you mean."

I am an avid fan of comedy, including the art of improvisation. One of the most fundamental rules of "improv" is the tactic known as "yes-anding." This means that each performer builds on what his co-performer has said. It is one of the core elements to creating engaging and immersive interaction between the performers. Improvisation artists are taught never to fizzle a scene with the concept of "no." That's not to say that One-on-One artists are restricted from saying "no." What "yes-anding" teaches us is that we can leverage what the student says in order to build up to where you ultimately want them to end up. This can take on many forms.

For example, suppose you ask your student to go over every rock formation he can remember. He may say, "Ok, so there are those volcanic rocks, then there are the layered rocks like in the Grand Canyon, and also those rocks that change and move from place to place." You could respond with, "Yes, those volcanic rocks you mentioned are called 'igneous' rocks, then the layered rocks of the Grand Canyon are called 'sedimentary' rocks, and finally those changing rocks are appropriately named 'metamorphic' rocks. Let's discuss each further." Notice how the One-on-One instructor can leverage the student's language to bind what that student already knows with what she needs to know.

The isolative nature of learning cannot be overstressed. The feeling of not understanding or underperforming, especially in the direct presence of a One-on-One teacher, can be nerve-racking for the student. Therefore, a great way to build bridges and communicate that you understand him is to say, "I know what you mean" when appropriate. For instance, many students see what should be read as, "x squared" and instead refer to it as, "x two." In order to point out this mistake, say, "I know what you mean when you say x two. Want to try resaying it the correct way?" Now, the student can feel that you understand him. You frame yourself as an ally and partner through this statement. It gives him a chance to rectify his mistake without perceiving any judgment in the process. Saying, "I know what you mean," both in this educational context, as well as in general, is a colossal interpersonal gift of compassion and empathy.

Start where they are

Each person needs to begin the learning journey at a point of crystal clear understanding. Better yet, not only can One-on-

One masters begin from a point of student understanding, but also from a point of student *interest*. For example, if a student is learning how to write a character analysis, ask him to choose someone he knows or who inspires him. Or if a student needs to understand percentages, and you know she is interested in basketball, discuss highly relevant topics such as free throws percentages, win-to-loss ratios, or anything else that piques her interest.

Take some time to set up the learning example. Starting from a point of student understanding and/or interest is an *immersive* act. It's not just cutesy space-filler for you to quickly insert whatever lesson you originally had in mind. Take a little time to discuss that particular person who inspires your student, or how important the aspect of free throws is in basketball. The only risk of this immersive approach is that it may sidetrack some students. He or she may much rather talk about basketball and find it difficult to return to the concept at hand. Should that happen, mentally note that taking a moment to paint the picture of a real-life example may not work for that particular student. By and large though, many students appreciate a One-on-One teacher's efforts to personalize learning to concepts and themes that register best in the students' minds. Fusing new learning with existing knowledge and interests has the potential to instill in your students lifelong understanding.

"Pause. Play."

Diving into lengthy reading is a daunting task that intimidates many students. They see several paragraphs in a row, perhaps in reading comprehension exercises or math word problems, and cringe. Perhaps the whole exercise bores them, or the passage doesn't make sense, or the subject is far-removed from their personal frame of reference. From the outset, ask the student to begin reading, so that you can get a sense of whether he is initially grasping the passage's meaning. Then ask the student to pause at certain intervals you deem worthy of follow-up or discussion. This maneuver is a great way to help your student relate to the text.

Pausing has several positive effects. For one, it breaks up the monotony. Your student can come up for air and avoid the trance-like state that many students experience while reading. That same "trance" happens occasionally with me too. It's the feeling of reading the words while simultaneously having no idea of what's going on. After your student reads a few sentences, say, "pause" as a check in. From here, you can inquire in two directions: the past or the future.

You can look into the past by asking, "Ok, what was the main idea of what you just read?" Or you can peek into the future by asking, "So, what do you expect to see next?" Inquiring about the passage's main ideas prompts your student to fully commit to the words he has already read. Interestingly, you may notice that when you ask your student about a main idea, he'll actually go back and reread with a hyper-engaged eye. Summarization is a skill that "pausing" invites. Thankfully, a fancy summary is usually unnecessary. He can say something to the effect of, "This guy studied rock formations and believes that the earth's age can be figured out by them." If your student struggles to summarize what he just read, then help him go back into the text and look for the main ideas, sentence by sentence.

Express to him that summarization skills require practice, and that he'll definitely become more comfortable by undertaking this process more.

On the other hand, asking the student about what he expects to see ahead fosters an ownership of the author's message(s). Critical reading is never passive. Give your student plenty of opportunities to create big-picture realizations for himself. He may say, "So another scientist was just mentioned, so it'll probably talk about how her views differ from the first guy's." The good news is that your student's hypothesis need not be right. The mere creation of a hypothesis is all that matters. Either your student's theory will be confirmed, or the author will throw in a surprise. Regardless of how the text plays out, now your student is looking for insights and answers that he might not have sought out if he had not paused to hypothesize. If your student struggles to predict what may come next, work together to build that skill in him. Teach him to look for clues, key words, tone, and pertinent data. When both of you are sufficiently ready to move on to the next parts of the passage, say, "Play."

This pause-to-play method works for any reading, including the infamously loathed math word problems (cue sinister music). Below is a sample dialogue that might occur between you and your student, in which you help her pin down the text and then own the problem using her intuition and common sense.

You: "So just start by reading it please, and we'll check in along the way."

Student: "Marie has a pizza restaurant that for lunch serves individual pizza slices and cans of soda."

Covering the rest of the passage with your hand, you say: "Pause. So what kind of information do you think is coming next?"

Student: "They'll probably talk about the prices of each."

You: "Sounds good, ok, play."

Student continues and smiles when she sees her prediction is right: "Each slice costs $3 and each soda costs $1. Yesterday, Marie made $100. She sold a total of 40 slices and sodas combined."

You, again covering the rest of the passage: "Pause. Ok so lots of information was just given. What do we know?"

Student: "Ok well, Marie's selling pizzas and sodas. We know how much each costs. And we know how much money she made, which is $100, and..." reading through it again, "... that a total of 40 of everything was sold."

You: "Rock on. Now, what do you think they'll ask about next?"

Student hesitates.

You continue: "If you were selling pizza and soda during a lunch hour, besides prices, what information would be crucial to know?"

After a few seconds of deep thought, student says: "Oh! How many of each?"

You: "Are you sure?"

Student: "Yes."

You: "Bingo. Ok, play."

Student reads while nodding and smiling: "How many slices and sodas each did Marie sell yesterday?"

Notice that during the dialogue, you ask questions relating to both the past and the future. Asking "what do we know?" is a past-oriented question, whereas asking, "what will they ask about?" looks ahead to the future of the passage. In this scenario, you require your student to conquer each section before moving on, both in terms of understanding what she has read, as well as predicting what comes next. You also bring the information to life in your student's mind, asking her to become the restaurateur and think like a businessperson. Leave no stone unturned until you're convinced that your student understands enough to "play" out the rest of the passage.

The pause-to-play imagery, akin to how we control virtually every video/audio device, creates a familiar feeling for your student. Familiarity breeds comfort, and all of a sudden, your reading experience together is monumentally improved. Over time, convey to your student how important it is for her to pause *herself* while reading. Instill within her the notion of creating an inner dialogue while reading, similar to the external dialogue you shared when working through the previous pizza word problem example.

The phobia of lengthy reading is rooted in the fear of being lost. Your job is to impart essential comprehension skills onto your student, such that the purpose of the passage takes shape within her mind. Pausing to check in happens frequently and naturally in social settings. We have no qualms about asking someone to repeat what was said or to clarify. Apply that same principle, explicitly, to the written word too.

Admit when you're wrong or confused

If you make a mistake, then immediately own it. Model optimal learning behavior for your student, as such behavior bears life-altering promise. Think about it: every respected employer, employee, teacher, parent, spouse, and friend takes responsibility for mistakes that they make. By owning mistakes, you let your student experience what it feels like to be on the receiving end of such high emotional maturity.

When some educators take part in One-on-One learning, they feel as if they must have all the solutions, correctly, every time. Given the highly immersive style of One-on-One instruction I advocate for in this book, we must acknowledge that being spot-on at every juncture is not realistic. Taking immediate ownership of our mistakes removes the stigma associated with those mistakes and thankfully reframes mistake-making as just another component of learning.

We must assume that our expertise and subject experience render our mistakes relatively seldom. If you ever come to a point in which you are confused or out of your league, that's OK. Try saying the following, "I'm fine with everything up to this point, but this new section here is giving me trouble. What I can do is…" (propose some plan that will rectify the confusion, whether it be researching it online, or in a book, or promising to look into it and return to the student with the answer). Remember, some mistakes and confusion are reasonable, and they can be leveraged both to reduce the aforementioned stigmatization with mistakes, as well as to reinforce the collaborative nature of One-on-One learning and remind the student that master teachers never let their egos get in the way. Should confusion arise too often for comfort, though, the time has come to offer your student several alternative plans to ensure he gets the help he needs. Bear in mind: students know the precise moment when we're in over our heads, and that moment usually occurs simultaneously to when *we* figure that out as well. Address that figurative elephant roaring in the room by bringing the truth to the forefront. Better to say, "I don't know" with integrity than to falsify knowing.

Chapter 5

NOT TO-DO'S

N ow here are some directed strategies for what the One-on-One artist should do to avoid pitfalls.

Food for thought? Not really.

There is something very appealing about the idea of munching on a snack in the learning setting. It creates an informal atmosphere, and food increases the energy that the body and brain need in order to learn. However, the cost of having food present is too great to enjoy its advantages. Food distracts, period. This is especially true if the food requires utensils or can easily get messy. If so, such a scenario would require the student to clumsily switch between writing and eating utensils, over and over again. Learners cannot take the greatest strides possible when dealing with any distractions, and food is definitely one of those.

Remember, we are taking part in the timeless tradition of One-on-One mentoring/advising/instructing. I doubt that in the middle of an intensive strategy session between Michael Jordan and coach Jackson did Jordan start unwrapping a Subway sandwich. Nor in the throes of explaining an intricate new feature in Apple software did founders Steve Wozniak and Steve Jobs repeatedly pop grapes into their mouths in front of their technical team, or vice versa. The learning exchange must be honored. Besides, I contend that the food loses its taste and is not as enjoyable when the brain simultaneously must maintain a high level of attention to a cerebral task. Eating loses its intention and descends into mindless chewing and swallowing. I acknowledge that sometimes eating is unavoidable, such as during lunch meetings. However whenever possible, find ways to eat before or after the learning window, which will not only honor the learning, but also honor the eating.

Sarcasm is SO AWESOME.

As in, it's not. In truth, I am a sarcasm connoisseur. I love a good sarcastic quip. With rare exceptions, though, I nix the sarcasm while deep in the learning. The act of learning requires high vulnerability on the students' part. They are opening themselves up to possible embarrassment, or even worse, to outright failure. That mode of entrenched learning has no room for potentially misconstrued jokes. Stick to being pleasant. Funny is good, energetic is good, informality is good. But leave it there. Any remark that runs even the smallest risk of offending your student is one to stay away from.

Note that I'm referring only to sarcasm as it applies to the learning exchange, not within normal communication parameters. If you and your student are sitting near a window and a fire truck siren blares outside for example, then it's ok to say with sarcastically dry panache, "That siren needs to be louder." Humor breaks the ice, and sarcasm is one arm of humor. With regard to the learning at hand, though, remain literal. Your student needs you to be.

Talk to my agent.

One-on-One learning is a contract between you and your student. Other parties can be critical, such as parents, family members, counselors, employers, administrators, coaches, other teachers, and/or anyone else in a peripheral supporting role. However, those other players are around solely to support, not to overly involve themselves in the sacred learning relationship. As you are the One-on-One authority figure, protect the learning relationship from others' over-involvement. Here are some examples of over-involvement:

- Parents dictating that their child get additional help without the child's input or consent. Students must be included in any decision related to them, including seeking One-on-One support. If the child does not want the support, but the parent deeply feels she needs it, the conversation should focus on understanding why the child feels as she does and working to bridge the gap between their stances.

- A school counselor who communicates with the student's teacher about classroom matters that should be resolved ideally between the teacher and student directly. These matters may include course difficulties, grade discrepancies, and challenges with the workload. The counselor should advise the student on how to advocate for himself directly to the teacher, assist the student in learning life skills such as time management, and only get involved with class-related matters if any breakdown in communication occurs.

- Parents who have sole control over their child's scheduling. Within reasonable parameters that the parents lay out, age-appropriate students must have a real say regarding the meetings, as in where, how often, and for how long. Student voices matter.

- Teachers who get offended or threatened when students seek outside help. Anything those teachers do from that point on risks undercutting the One-on-One potential. Their adverse reaction proves that their ego is involved, which has no place here. No single party should ever own learning.

As the One-on-One consultant, involve your student as much as possible in all matters regarding her: scheduling, progress reports, goals discussions, and action plans. As diplomatically as possible, convey to others in the vicinity that you are beholden to your student, first and foremost. Agents, on the other hand, may have an agenda.

Let's talk about praise. By the way, for reading this book I think you're amazing.

I give you a lot of credit for wanting to improve your One-on-One craft. The continual quest to improve must be essential throughout our lives; therefore, seeking to do so isn't entirely praiseworthy. It is worthy of *respect* though. Let's distinguish between doling out lots of praise and offering a high amount of respect. I respect you for wanting to learn more. I respect our students for wanting to learn more as well. Herein lies the critical difference: *praise must be saved for what is praiseworthy, while respect is a way of life.*

Leading research in child development backs this concept. Author Alfie Kohn cites University of Northern Iowa education professor Rheta DeVries in her assertion that praise, in its constant usage as a positive feedback tool designed to instigate desired results, is nothing more than "sugar-coated control." Sometimes we get so obsessed with reinforcing student behaviors that we lose sight of all the depth and uniqueness inherent within each individual. Dishing out (or withholding) praise can be a form of non-presence. Put another way, every choice and process the student undertakes down his unique path to comprehension, including mistakes, lose their built-in value when educators laser their focus into what is or is not praiseworthy. Each student's unique path is the *entire point* of learning. Learning is about self-discovery. The praise game blinds us to their self-discovery process, rendering us non-present to where and who they are.

Parents can be notorious for this. Suppose a father wants to teach his child the act of folding laundry. The parent who fixates on praising what he deems as the "correct" set of actions loses sight of the crucial notion that *how* the child learns this act must be left entirely up to that child. Waiting to pounce on actions to either approve or disapprove of is manipulative, despite the parent's best intentions to teach the child "the right way to do it." Using or withholding praise to compel a student to behave as we wish dilutes what is actually a complex human being into little more than a puppet performing a series of empty, prescribed actions.

The praise game grooms young people to expect high volumes of complimentary statements like "good job!" for their behavior. Fittingly, such continual external feedback blurs the *intrinsic* (internal) motivators that should naturally drive their pursuit of growth and success.

Picture a young child working on a painting. Her teacher could say, "Wow, that's amazing! You're such a good painter." But *is* the painting amazing, or *is* the child a really good painter? If the child is not "such a good painter," we might wonder if the teacher is complimenting her artwork because he is afraid of deflating her fragile ego. If so, will this flattering statement plant false realities in the child's mind? Will she be able to handle constructive criticism later in life if the lion's share of feedback she receives now is all praise-centered (and not necessarily merited at that)? Or worse yet, will she consciously or unconsciously expect to hear praise whenever she paints, then eventually lose interest when no one directly gives it to her?

What if instead her teacher says, "Wow, you worked hard on this! I see you used a lot of blue, with more green over here." Let's closely examine this approach. "Wow, you worked hard!" is positive in nature. It bases the positivity of the sentiment on the concept of work. Crediting the work in and of itself with words like "wow" and "nice" is appropriate. The teacher's next statement is where the interaction can *really* begin. She does not indiscriminately seek out something else to praise, rather she discusses what is unequivocally true, in this case, the child's choice of colors. This methodology has two major benefits. First, it does not falsely inflate the child's ego. Second, it opens the door to the real magic: a connective discussion as to *why* the child chose those colors, what she likes about them, what colors she has chosen for different pieces, etc. In other words, a meaningful, two-way dialogue based on what truly exists is the ultimate key to the student's growth, far more than a one-size-fits-all rah-rah-rah.

Dr. Carol Dweck, renowned Stanford psychology professor and author of the groundbreaking book *Mindset,* reports on what drives motivation within us. She distinguishes between two mindsets: the fixed mindset and the growth mindset. A person who has a fixed mindset believes that all success emanates from one's individual talents and abilities, which he/she believes to be generally static during one's life. A person who has a growth mindset, on the other hand, operates from the belief that intelligence and skills can be developed with persistent efforts.

A critical element of Dweck's different mindsets regards the use of praise. Praising a student's achievements based on intelligence, e.g. saying, "You're so smart!" after he earns an "A" on a test in fact *promotes* the fixed mindset. The implied lesson to the student is that every success (and failure) has less to do with his effort and more to do with his natural abilities. The student will consequently be more risk averse and more fearful of failure, which comes with the threat of rendering the student stupid in his own eyes. In contrast, praising a student's hard work leads that student to generate a growth mindset, whereby success and failure are attributable to effort, which we have far greater control over than intelligence.

I applaud Dweck's work on mindsets, as I believe it to be life changing. I have some critical reservations about the praise component of her theories, though. When we try to develop the growth mindset in students by praising their hard work, we mustn't get wrapped up in formulaically trying to sway our student's individual *process* in one direction or another. Wouldn't an incessant focus on a student's level of hard work, even in the valiant goal of instigating a growth mindset, also be a sugar-coated form of controlling that student? We must let students exist as they are.

Let's return to the example of the painting child. Mapping out a praise strategy based on hard work misses the larger point. I believe that the correct approach centers on creating a rich, meaningful, and emotionally resonant connection with the young artist. Learn what matters to her, what she thinks of and feels while painting, and act as a mirror of wisdom and understanding on her journey. In that connective space, any talk of fixed or growth mindsets will evaporate. Only the teacher and the student exist, together on a higher energetic plane. Hypothetically, if the student makes an astute observation and the teacher replies with, "Wow, I like how your mind works," this response would be considered a faux pas in Dweck's view because it constitutes praising intelligence. But I contend that this response is fine; it's wonderful, in fact! The response emanates directly from the moment at hand. The student just offered a noteworthy insight, so the teacher, present to that moment, comments on the student's mind from a connective human level. Such overtures to connect trump any discussion of how to influence the student's actions through specific types of praise. Technically speaking, the teacher's response *is* a form of praise. What makes the exchange so positive is not whether the teacher offers praise, or what kind of praise it is for: hard work or intelligence. Rather, the positivity of the exchange stems from the teacher being *present* enough to the moment to offer such a timely, intuitive response to the student's statement.

Once we arrive in the One-on-One zone, I maintain that we must have the freedom to be open with our words, whether they are designed to praise something specific or to engage in candid discussion. Or we can simply do away with our words and just plain listen. To be clear, I agree with Dweck that intelligence and capabilities are not fixed; they grow with sustained efforts. However, her views on the types of praise and their respective effects should never overshadow the reality that teacher-student interactions are complex, unscripted, and when fully connective, immune from pre-determined notions of praise "A" being better than praise "B." Do you wish to establish authentic growth within your students, both in their mindset and in their lives? Connect with who they are as people; that is the ultimate key.

Think of the people with whom you feel most connected. These individuals are those whom you listen to with intent, whom you would change for, and whom you wish to please. Chances are that such a connection did not arise out of a praise-based interaction. As educators, we yearn for that deep connection, which we know will inspire transcendent student performance. Mistakenly, though, many well-intentioned educators dish out praise like tacos on Taco Tuesday. What they don't realize is that their over-praising makes the student "over" their praising. In other words, excessive praise causes the student to value their compliments less highly. By the Law of Diminishing Returns, each successive offer of praise minimizes the impact of every future offer. Saying "great job!" to everything, such as standard progress, minimizes the impact of saying "great job!" for the hard-earned "A" on a test. Praise, indeed, *is* tempting to pour on, because it sounds wonderful coming out and the student easily digests it… at first. However over time, it foments a quiet inner turmoil within the student. The turmoil tries to call out, "I should not be receiving all this praise for merely doing what I need to do!"

Save the praise for that which is actually praiseworthy. Encouragement and respect are our motivational tools during the learning phase, while praise is what we save for the end, if/when the student rises to the occasion and delivers. Praiseworthy feats are events in line with strong grades on exams/projects, solid long-term work habits, major improvements, sustained effort and maturity, altruism/consideration for others, etc. Standard, non-praiseworthy responsibilities are on par with doing homework, paying attention, being on time, being respectful/pleasant, doing what is expected, incremental growth as it naturally occurs, etc.

Final disclaimer: I'm a really nice guy. By nature, I'm encouraging, and I definitely look for ways to catch a student when she does something right and point that out to her. If halfway through the lesson she becomes stressed by the difficulty, but nevertheless successfully works through the problems, then I'll say, "You're doing well" to affirm that I see her persistent efforts. But I don't start with that statement from the outset, and I certainly don't repeat it again for a little while, maybe only once at the end if necessary. On the other hand, throughout the lesson I *do* offer encouragement, steeped in a tone of respect, including feedback such as, "Yes, go for it, correct, you got it, way to find your own mistake, seems like you're getting this, good question, you're asking the right questions, almost... think again, you know what to do here," etc. One-on-One masters create a positive, professional dynamic. Learning is all in a day's work, so it doesn't really deserve that much praise. But once you witness your student using that learning to accomplish something significant, then any honest praise you give will be well-received and highly appreciated.

Chapter 6

WHEN IT GOES WRONG, PERMANENTLY ENDING FOUR LEVELS OF STUDENT SHUTDOWN

S ometimes students forget the big picture. They lose sight of why you sit with them, why they should exert full effort, and what the point of it all is. This is almost always non-malicious; they just need guidance to get back on track. Here are four scenarios that every One-on-One artist will eventually need to address with both immediacy and sensitivity, presented in increasing intensity levels. Without confronting each type of challenge head-on and resolving them in partnership, we invite the risk of student shutdown—another cold killer of inspired learning.

Level 1: When students are stressed

Dr. Madeline Levine, in her fantastic book, *Teach Your Children Well*, writes of the huge prevalence of academic stress in students' lives. Her research shows that while in the past, problems with friends and family have been the main stressors; now students cite school as their highest source of stress. She goes on to list the daunting array of factors that contribute to students' overall stress: "stress, exhaustion, depression, anxiety, poor coping skills, an unhealthy reliance on others for support and direction, and a weak sense of self." If we notice our students checking out or shutting down, we are duty-bound not to sweep their behavior under the rug. We are hyper-aware, tuned-in mentors, looking out for them at all times. So, seize the moment to reach out and connect. A simple, "Are you ok?" does *wonders*. People just want to be seen, to feel that they matter, so checking in with your students on a human level cuts right to their core. Simply knowing that you care for their well-being is oftentimes the best way to help them snap out of any temporary funk.

Not only do people want to be seen, but they also want to be heard. Within reason, and not as a rule, your student may just need a few moments to describe to you how much she is dealing with these days. Keep in mind that it's ok for students to clear their head through an occasional, reasonable vent, in the spirit of establishing synchronicity with you. It's not ok for them to hijack One-on-One time and turn it into a complaining scene more suited for reality TV. Should a student's vent go too far or too often, gently reel her back in, acknowledge what you heard her say, and move forward together. While we may never know the full picture, it is our job to get as much of our students' stories as possible. If you believe your student is too overwhelmed by the gauntlet of everyday life in or out of school, then by all means let her support network know. Too much stress and inspired learning are mutually exclusive.

Level 2: When students are disenchanted

Remember the feeling of being in a course that you found utterly boring/disheartening/unsatisfying/useless? When your student experiences this, your role in the situation has profound ramifications. Play it right, and you may be your student's sole beacon of hope and joy amidst a terrible class experience. Play it wrong, and you will be lumped right in with the course content/experience your student so despises. I have seen firsthand how masters of course material did not achieve One-on-One mastery because they failed to separate themselves from the material or situation when necessary. Thus, should a student ever find a subject or situation disenchanting, and should the One-on-One educator fail to take the time to acknowledge the student's feelings or discuss the big picture, then that student will merely see the educator as another extension of the subject and will subsequently write that educator off. Here's a dialogue showcasing how to resolve this dilemma and come out on top:

"Brian, is something the matter?"

"No, not really. I just don't really like this stuff. Chemistry isn't really my thing."

"I can understand that. Is it an issue of being hard for you?"

"That's part of it. But even when I do get it, I'm like 'eh'."

(Nod/smile appropriately to acknowledge his feelings.) "Of course. It would be unrealistic to expect all students to love every course they take. And I think that in general, all of us should try to only take courses from which we genuinely want to learn more. So I imagine that you *have* to take this course, for some transcript reason?"

"Yeah, it sucks."

"And you're here now, and we're sitting here. To me, it seems then that our goal should be to just move through it together and get you to the other side successfully. Does that sound fair to you?"

"Yeah, no, I get that. I just gotta do it, I suppose."

"Yes, there are plenty of things we all need to do sometimes, some of which aren't inspiring. I know that feeling and I've been there. Chemistry actually is a field of study which I personally find inspiring, just like the zillions of fields out there that many people find inspiring: music, languages, math, sports, engineering, art, dance. Chemistry is the study of the most basic building blocks of life that make up everything—you, me, this pencil, our whole world. I'm not saying you should fall in love with it. I'm just saying that you're here now, and this is a chance for you to just learn about another field of study that's out there. You're basically exposing your brain to something new, which you otherwise would never be exposed to."

"That makes sense for sure. I guess it's just weird that I'm *forced* to take it."

"Yeah I agree. Being forced isn't a great way to learn."

This dialogue holds many undercurrents. It begins with the One-on-One instructor spotting an issue with Brian and opening the door to give him a voice in the matter. Then the instructor acknowledges Brian's feelings about not liking chemistry, rather than glossing over his feelings or immediately trying to convince him not to have them. Most importantly, the instructor framed him/herself as Brian's teammate by saying, "We'll get through it together." At that point, Brian was ready to move on. He said, "I just gotta do it." Moving on would be fine at this point, but here, the One-on-One instructor seizes the opportunity to turn this ordinary moment into a *big picture* moment. The instructor speaks his/her truth about loving chemistry, about chemistry's place amongst the numerous fields of study out there, and sums the subject up in a compelling, macro nutshell by referring to chemistry as "the study of the most basic building blocks of life." Then the instructor gives Brian further acknowledgement/empathy regarding being forced to learn it.

I believe in understanding your student's perspective. But in the process of understanding him, don't lose sight of your values. Attempting to be chummy with your student by collectively disparaging the subject material does not appeal to a higher standard. If you think chemistry is awesome, then say so, even if your student hates it. But only do so while simultaneously granting your student the equal right to have less positive views of the subject you have come to love. This way, you may actually convince your student indirectly that chemistry *is* pretty awesome, through both your passion for it as well as your <u>absence of agenda</u> to persuade him of its awesomeness.

Level 3: When students are problematic

These are the times when students consciously or unconsciously undermine your attempts to create One-on-One synergy. Do not pretend to be oblivious. Call every action out that you believe may be eroding the learning environment you're working so hard to create.

Once I had a student who would liberate her hand from her pencil at *any* opportunity. When a problem was done, or halfway done, or even a quarter way done, or at the slightest whiff of frustration or difficulty, she would either whack the pencil down in irritation or let it tumble out of her hand in defeat. I went through Levels 1 and 2 with her, trying to figure out what was holding her back. It turned out that it was a little of everything: fatigue, stress, not liking the subject, early failures, being forced to take it, and who knows what else going on at home. But acknowledging her feelings did not resolve her conduct. So I said, "I know you're frustrated. I'm here to help you learn it so that you're less frustrated. Please don't drop the pencil all the time." It would get better for a little while, then the pencil liberation would resume. I tried some humor, "So I'm giving you a ration of three pencil drops from now until we're finished, so use them wisely." That didn't work either, but I still didn't let it go. I became more direct, asking plainly, "Sarah, are you intentionally trying to sidetrack us?"

This last question is very strategic. First, it does not let her behavior go unaddressed, thereby setting the standard for how the sessions should be run. Second, it gives Sarah an out so that she can still rectify her behavior and save face. It is much worse to intentionally disrupt than to unintentionally do so. My question communicated to her that I was on to her shenanigans, but afforded her a backdoor to escape from. She replied, "No, no, no, I'm sorry, it's just so harrrd," which was the crack in her armor I needed to eventually learn about her fear of letting everyone down. Once we could communicate about her fear and alleviate it somewhat, we were able to resume our positive working environment.

Effective systems by which we communicate are vital to a successful One-on-One interaction. Keep those bi-directional systems intact, and the learning will dramatically increase as a result. Be friendly, be kind, be sensitive, be a pro, and never be a doormat. Call out everything you perceive to be getting in the way.

Level 4: When students are impossible

The worst situation we can encounter is when a student simply does not want One-on-One time. Maybe a parent or administrator forced him into it. Or perhaps meeting with you is part of some arrangement he needs to abide by in order to rectify another issue either directly or indirectly related. For example, maybe he was unilaterally told, "Part of your academic probation requires you to meet with your teacher every Thursday" or "You need to meet with this person or you won't be allowed to be on the wrestling team." This is a hard situation for both participants in the One-on-One relationship. From the student's perspective, he has not actively chosen to receive help; rather, help has been mandated to him. From the One-on-One instructor's perspective, squandering valuable time with someone who dreads coming and who can't wait to leave violates the timeless and sacred apprenticeship bond.

In these situations, often the damage has already been done. Performance is low, motivation is lower, and morale is virtually non-existent. This is the time to take four or five large figurative steps back together and fully synchronize with your student. Take a lot of time to fully immerse with her; it's quite possible that many people in her life have not. Empathize. If you have ever struggled mightily at an endeavor, then you know how devastating it can be on your psyche. Now imagine adding circumstances that would remove all self-determination from your action plan. Sometimes we do just that to our students, forcing them to rectify their problems on terms that they don't consent to, such as mandated teacher/tutor meetings or unilateral decisions without their input. Consequently, is it any wonder why a student in this position would be standoffish, apathetic, or bitter?

Work to understand the full scope of why your student feels the way she does. Then reframe the situation, using any chance to offer genuine life perspective. Discuss the big picture. Such a move will direct her mind away from obsessing about her situation and towards more productive thoughts. Most likely, many interpersonal dynamics have been in the works long before you enter the scene. This is your opportunity to create a fresh dynamic with your student, separate from the pre-existing power struggles or ongoing despair. The dynamic you generate must live and breathe under the banner of *partnership* with your student. In age-appropriate ways, *involve her* in these major decisions going on in her life, and advocate on her behalf when reasonable.

The following is a sample dialogue with one such down-and-out student:

"Wow, that sounds really tough, taking Algebra for a third time."

"Yeah, it sucks, but whatever, I guess."

"What do you mean by 'whatever'?"

The student may discuss a variety of explanations as to why the need to retake the course again happened. Some explanations are her responsibility to bear, such as her not fully committing to the class, giving inconsistent effort, having poor time management, or making faulty prioritization choices. Still other reasons contributing to her difficulty may have been out of her hands, such as having ineffective teachers in her past, experiencing problems at home, or living within unsupportive communities and networks.

"That doesn't sound like 'whatever' to me, it sounds like your life." Now it's time to directly respond to what she just said. If her reasons stem from choices that were her responsibility, you can add, "Well clearly you had a lot going on. And I think having a life rich with activities is a wonderful thing. Still, all of us have our responsibilities. I give you a lot of credit for standing up and owning what you need to do by taking the class again, even though it's taking longer than you'd like." Or, if her reasons were not her fault, you could sympathize by saying, "I agree that any teacher who actually yells at students needs to figure out better ways to communicate. They're the leaders, and they should inspire." (Caveat: some students fabricate their plight. I believe in beginning from a place of trust though. Your primary job is to acknowledge her perspective.) After you mirror back some authentic acknowledgement of her situation, you can begin to re-direct her attention to solving her problem. "Still, here we are," you say. "What do you think needs to be done about it?"

"Doesn't matter what I think, my mom is forcing me to do this."

"So first of all, it *does* matter what you think. Secondly, we're not just going to do this stuff without your buy-in. We won't just go through the motions, even if you've been forced to. That's not what this is all about, and it's certainly not what I'm about. So I just want to know, from you, what you think we should do?"

"I mean, I know I need to see you every week. But I've been through this before. I suck at math, I'm not going to need this in real life, so there's just no point to me."

"Emma, what really sucks more anything is the feeling of *not knowing* the math. I'm sure the idea of 5+5=10 doesn't suck for you. But if you want me to admit that you don't need to use square roots in daily life, at the grocery store or gas station, then absolutely, I agree. We have this system, it's called 'school,' and it's our society's far-less-than-perfect way of figuring out how you will handle yourself in your life. What we're trying to figure out is simple: how well do you respond to challenges? School throws these different challenges at you in the form of different subjects, and sooner or later, one of them is going to trip you up. For you, it's math. For me in high school, it was European history. Every task in life has at least some people for which it's hard. How you respond to each challenge reveals a lot about your character. We want to know, can you rise to the challenge? Hopefully, but can you rise to the challenge while also being a leader? Or playing a sport? Or playing an instrument? The act of committing to a process that's very difficult is exactly what makes us responsible adults. Wouldn't you want to hire someone who could commit to figuring something out, even if they found it hard or unappealing?"

Emma pauses to let in that you don't care as much about teaching her math than you do about teaching her how to live. "Yes, that's important, I can get that."

"I'm glad. We've all had to push through things we didn't enjoy, myself included. The hope is that over time during your life, you can position yourself to do the things you love and minimize the things you don't. Like me right now, I really enjoy doing this, being here with you. Over the course of my life, I've done plenty of work that I didn't find appealing. But this is *your* life, so what's *your* plan?"

"I need to meet with you every week."

"Yes, that was the plan given to you. And I'm sorry if you never had a say in it. But you realize that if anyone, you, me, anyone, was really behind on something, then it makes the most sense for that person to get consistent help on it while catching up."

"Yeah, I know."

"So are Thursdays good for you?"

"Actually I was thinking Mondays would be better because I could get ready for the week more easily that way."

If this schedule change works for your schedule and is logistically feasible for all parties, you can then agree, "Mondays are fine with me. Now that we have the day figured out, for us to be successful, I'll need to give you practice work between our sessions, so that you will keep improving and also will be able to come in with questions. Does that make sense?"

"Yes."

"About how many problems per week do you think would be appropriate?"

She is taken aback at the level of involvement being offered. "I don't know, I guess it would depend on the type of problems."

"That's true, fair enough. So what if at the end of each session, we decide together how many problems would be good for that week, cool?"

"Sure."

"Look, I know I said it already, but I know it's tough. I hope you realize that I want exactly what you want: for you to get over this thing, to be able to put it behind you, and to move on with your life. We need to create a program for you in order to do that, and the program can only exist by us seeing eye-to-eye, each step of the way. Ok? So shall we start?"

This is One-on-One mentorship at its finest. The instructor takes the student from standoffish to collaborative, from zero involvement to major involvement. Before learning any math, Emma takes a mental break from her situation and first takes a journey through the instructor's views on commitment and character. *For students who are not initially on board, before discussing any actual material, the One-on-One artist must find some common notion on which to forge a bridge, ideally by appealing to a higher cause. Too few teachers realize this vital concept, and jump into the learning prematurely.*

Following the fresh attunement established with Emma, the instructor is now free to create a plan-of-action with her, in an approach laced with respect and grounded in the spirit of partnership. In the above exchange, she and the instructor agree on a day together, collectively decide what kind of practice sets they will use together, and come to a common understanding of the need to collaborate to create a program. Keep in mind that the instructor already knows how many problems per week will be appropriate. Including Emma within that process, however, offers her *ownership* of the task at hand, because she has now committed her word to completing the work.

We must not underestimate the intrinsic yearning human beings have to make personal commitments and sense of satisfaction they experience when they work hard to achieve them. Author, speaker, and life coach Gayle Hilgendorff contends that people want to work hard when they first know (and agree on) exactly what they are working for. She goes on to say that hard work is optimal when such work enhances our lives and the lives of those around us.

We don't want to be hamsters running in place on a wheel. We all want to step up, work hard, and perform; we just need to be afforded the right circumstances in order to do so. Part of those circumstances for the student is the belief that her experiences, her voice, and her input *matter*. This way we, as One-on-One educators, can hold students accountable whenever they occasionally fall short of their obligations. We can remind them of our agreements, and since all transactions are bilaterally created, they have no excuse not to deliver. And most importantly, if they fail to succeed, we can point to their lack of following through on commitments, which is a much more manageable pill for them to swallow than defeatist statements such as "I'm just incapable/unlucky/dumb/etc." Here, Carol Dweck's mindset approach is highly pertinent. According to her, a student who fails and says, "I didn't work hard enough" has a much healthier and more resilient outlook than the student who fails and concludes in despair, "I'm just not smart enough."

On a final note, we must discuss the certain scenario that follows all our attempts to forge bridges, in which the student still refuses to buy in. A student can be sitting right beside you, but you know full well that he's miles away. I have always known the right course of action when this occurs, although I have only developed the courage to start implementing it in recent years. This course of action is simply not to work with the student.

Let's say I tried synchronizing with him, understanding him, offering him the perspective of the big picture, including him in the process, and creating a team atmosphere, and all of these strategies have missed the mark. Or repeatedly, he has not come through on his agreements, offering excuse after excuse. This type of conduct gone uncorrected negates the One-on-One contract. At this time, it is necessary to refuse to work with him. This action is never about being angry with the student, although a degree of sadness is sometimes applicable. Such sadness is expressed in the following sentiment, which you might offer when explaining why you must terminate the relationship: "I really want to work with you, but we can't if you're not honoring the time and effort we spend on trying to help you." The student may hear this and snap out of it, ready to try once more, at the risk of losing you. Or he may actually lose you, reflect on it for a few days, then change his mind and reconnect with you on renewed terms. Or who knows how he will react. The point is, verbalizing the exact point at which you won't continue marks a line in the sand, centered on a fundamental issue of respect. That line establishes that your time and work are valuable, and that your expertise will not be exploited without full and positive cooperation. At the end of it all, the student just may not be ready for what you have to offer. He may need to make his own decisions without your involvement, and he may need to learn from possible failure.

The reason that it has taken me years to implement the policy of walking away when necessary is that I have been grappling with my own insecurities. Will my student hate me? Am I abandoning him? Maybe he'll be better next time (even after five straight broken promises)? All of these are internal questions that I have dealt with whenever the inkling to back away has arisen in my mind. Your process may include all, some, or none of these same inner conflicts, or even other ones. My personal growth came with the realization that what we do is holy work. It encompasses our entire being. Think of the level of commitment we sustain for each student while in session. We must be fully prepared to offer everything our students need, both subject-wise and interpersonally, during every single minute together with him/her. Bluntly speaking, we experience a slap in the face when at least some of that investment is not given back from the student. We have too much to do while we're still alive. Wasting our time, skills, and energy with those who are not ready for us is not one of them.

Chapter 7

EVERY TEACHING TOOL POSSIBLE
WHILE HAVING TAPE
OVER YOUR MOUTH

*"A teacher is never a giver of truth; he is a guide, a pointer
to the truth that each student must find for himself."*
–Bruce Lee

Have you ever asked someone a question that you know he heard, yet receive no response? You may begin to wonder what the other person is thinking or re-examine your own question or endure a variety of other doubts that begin popping into your mind. The point is that meaning lies *behind* the non-response. This fascinating concept forms the basis of many marvelous tactics you can utilize in your One-on-One artistry. So much in life is rooted in what is *not* said. In this chapter, we explore the long-studied yet ever-elusive methods we can definitively use to communicate, without having to say a word.

Why is non-verbal communication important while teaching? Done correctly, it is a powerful pedagogical methodology. First, it communicates a vibe in which every word you *do* speak becomes absolutely necessary. In other words, you save your speech only for when it's unquestionably required. Second, and more importantly, not speaking enables your student to establish and operate her own *internal* dialogue. Through this inner voice, she can eventually meander to her own conclusions, which will always lead to much more effective and permanent comprehension. This chapter will give you every tool possible that you can use, while figuratively having tape over your mouth, in order to maximize each opportunity to let your student's internal (and then external) voices become central.

Imagine the very old and wise monk, looking at you contemplatively. You timidly ask him a question, and he simply looks at you and smiles kindly. You pause to think for a while, and you arrive at your conclusion, which it turns out was within your grasp all along. By no means at all am I telling you to become a monk. I certainly don't wear robes and sandals during my sessions. I am merely saying that we can employ many interrelated non-verbal tactics that will elevate your practice to One-on-One wizardry.

The non-response

The first question posed at the beginning of this chapter broaches the idea of not immediately responding to some questions, which can be a highly successful strategy. Be careful, though. Only save your non-response for the following scenarios. In each scenario, I include follow-up ideas to maximize each exchange, all while focusing on a student-based process:

Try not immediately responding when:
You pose questions that you believe your student may already know the answer to, but is feeling hesitant to reply because he is experiencing a moment of self-doubt. If your student waits for a reply from you, try saying, "I'm intentionally not saying anything right now so that you can figure this one out" or "Do you need me to answer you? If so, I will."

Try not immediately responding when:
A student seems to be thinking out loud, which includes asking (himself) questions and appearing immersed in thought. Your presence here, remarkably, is crucial. You serve as a *witness* to his learning process. Your presence validates him and silently supports him. It lets him know that even though neither of you are directly conversing, he is not alone by any means. Try projecting that sense of positive presence to him while he grapples with his problem. Focus on what he writes in real-time, silently read along with him if he needs to

revisit a text, and make eye contact with him when he looks at you as the wheels in his mind churn something out. Holding that eye contact while he's deep in thought actually supports him during those several extra seconds he may need to reach his "aha!" moment. If you are even slightly uncomfortable with silence, then now is unequivocally the time to get over it. Your student needs you. Here, specifically, he needs your perceivable yet soundless backing while he is immersed in deep thought.

Try not immediately responding if:
Your student does not know the answer to the same question you have explained several times. If you ask again and he doesn't know, your momentary silence implicitly encourages him to pay attention to what has been previously covered. He may ask you a follow-up question. Some possible non-verbal reactions you could offer back are nodding as if to say, "Yes, that *is* the right question, so…" or lifting your eyebrows as if to say, "Yes, I'm waiting for you to know the answer to that" or turning your gaze to where a clue to the answer exists on the page. At some point, you must break the cycle of your student asking the same question over and over and shift the onus onto him to remember the answer.

Try not immediately responding if:
Your student asks you a question, then stumbles onto an idea, and immediately attempts to answer her own question. Clam up and let her try to figure it out, and only get involved if she is truly stuck. Take joy in witnessing your student's learning

journey. This is among the purest displays of the human experience we can ever behold.

Try not immediately responding if:
Your student asks you the wrong question. Not immediately responding will give your student a chance to reevaluate what she has just said. You could offer a contemplative glance, as if to say, "Hmmmm, try again" or cock your head to the side as if to say, "Well, think about what you just asked..." Either way, extend the life of this moment by non-verbally hinting that your student is on the wrong track in order to allow her a chance to rectify her approach. Get involved the instant you perceive her to be perpetuating the same mistake or if she is lost.

Referencing previous work
In chapter three, we discussed the merits of creating our own teaching program by starting from square one, on blank paper. This procedure usually involves crafting segway driven concepts that progressively increase in complexity. A positive aspect of this system is that you can mentally note where each concept resides on the pages, for use during later moments in the session, or even during later sessions.

Let's suppose a certain problem on the page stumps your student. She grapples with the snag, and you allow her some time to figure it out, yet she remains stuck. Without uttering a word, flip to the other side of the page, which reveals another problem she solved ten minutes ago, highly similar to the problem she is currently on. The student then says, "Oh!" and excitedly flips the page back and resumes working where she left off. Directly pointing to proof that she was already successful on a similar question does wonders for her sense of empowerment. Plus it fosters your student's ability to reference, read, and understand her own previous work. Students in rigorous high school and collegiate programs must develop the ability to learn from their notes, assignments, and graded materials. Modeling that technique and offering real exposure and practice for your students goes a long way towards developing that skill set.

The cover-up

Take a look at your fingers. Hopefully your nails are clean and well groomed, the skin unchapped. Because it's time to let your hands and fingers take the spotlight. As we immerse deeper and deeper into teaching our fields of expertise, the paper we use will become increasingly more packed with work. As your student forges on, look for moments when you need her to focus on one specific idea, section, or problem. To direct her focus, simply cover up anything else in the vicinity. This works great for a variety of situations, such as two-part concepts. By covering up one part of a problem at a time, you can make a silent hint as to where the hesitating student should proceed next in her work.

Here is an example of how to use this technique during an English grammar lesson in which you discuss how to avoid a "comma splice." Start by covering up every word after a comma and then bringing the student's attention to the word that follows it. If the word that follows is a conjunction (e.g. "and," "but," "or"), then everything that follows the conjunction should constitute an independent clause (i.e. a portion of the sentence that could stand as a sentence on its own). If there is no conjunction following the comma, then the sentence likely has a comma splice. If there is a conjunction following the comma, your next task is to reveal the words that follow in order to determine if they can serve as a stand-alone sentence, in which case there is no comma splice. To solidify the lesson, uncover everything in order to show how the comma coupled with "and" separate two fully formed sentences.

Step 1: Cover up everything following the comma, proving the first part of this sentence could be a sentence in and of itself.

Example: **We went to the deli,** ~~and we realized that every sesame bagel was sold out~~.

Step 2: Reveal the next word after the comma to see if it is a conjunction or not.

Example: We went to the deli, **and** ~~we realized that every sesame bagel was sold out~~.

Step 3: Cover the first part of the sentence, demonstrating that everything after ", and" can also be a sentence in and of itself.

Example: ~~We went to the deli,~~ and **we realized that every sesame bagel was sold out**.

The conclusion: This is a correct sentence with no comma splice, because the conjunction "and" separates two independent clauses.

This methodology can also work with digital screens. For example, when I help students prepare for the GRE, we work on laptops because the exam is computer adaptive. During one session, a problem appeared on the screen, which I quickly scanned before immediately covering up the answer choices by placing my hand one inch away from the screen. After my student read the problem, with my hand still covering up the answers, I asked, "What types of answers do you expect to see here?" Had I not covered up the answers, her eyes would have involuntarily darted to the answer list and begun rapidly assessing the options. This is known as "sight word reading," the ability to immediately recognize the identity of known words at the mere sight of those words, without necessarily reading them in the traditional way (Ehri). Once we have read words on impulse, we can't *un*-read them. Thus, covering up the answer choices before asking my question was essential.

The only way to conquer a daunting task is to approach it in small, manageable increments. Covering up certain components of a task so as to break it down into smaller steps directly decreases the chances that your student will be overwhelmed by the overall problem. Seeing everything at once can be overwhelming, but seeing one piece at a time and building from there is quite doable.

Think of the infomercial that aims to sell us a fancy new knife set. Meticulously, from beginning to end, the infomercial's producers have laid out each scene they want us to focus on, one in rapid succession after the other. The production may start with one small knife, involving a quick *ooh-ahh* demonstration of what it can do to an apple. Then another knife appears alongside the first, slightly bigger, and *wow*, see what it can do to this raw steak. Then another scene, another knife, another demonstration, more knives, cutting boards, and then the grand finale: double the entire offer to send the second knife set to your mom for Christmas. See what they do? They would never start the infomercial by urging you to "buy two complete sets," as that would come across as a turn-off. Instead, they start small, inviting you to focus on something more approachable: one small, sleek knife. In essence, the power of the infomercial is their ability to "cover up" what they ultimately have in store for you, until they deem you ready to experience the entire package. They take us on a very compelling, mesmerizing journey. We can use these tactics ourselves, as One-on-One specialists.

Take your student on a journey too, starting with just a single concept. Build and build, one increment at a time, until you eventually construct castles of understanding. Control what he sees at every opportunity. Use your hands deftly and smoothly to cover up anything along the way, either to crystallize what you're currently saying, or to silently *replace* any words you would need to use otherwise. Do this right, and by end of the session, you will see your student have that same look of wonder, a silent expression of, "Wow, how did we end up *here*?"—just like at the end of the infomercial when we ask in bewilderment, "Wow, why did I buy two knife sets again?"

Back to the basics

Once I asked a student, "What's $4x - x$?"

She answered incorrectly, "4."

I did not say a single word and kept my face neutral, so she wouldn't feel judged or self-conscious for missing a relatively straightforward question. I chose instead to write a series of successive statements, waiting for her to answer each one before writing the next. The progression is below. Keep in mind—I prefer not to speak much during these build-ups. A little affirmation here and there, or a simple "yes" after each right answer is fine. But as I discussed in the "Not To-Do's" chapter, I believe in saving praise for truly praiseworthy moments. Simple nods of respect or smiles are sufficient while your student traverses the small steps. Not speaking ensures that we don't cloud our students' inner compass.

When she couldn't answer $4x - x$, I wrote:

$4 - 1 =$

And she wrote: 3. Correct.

Then I wrote:

4 apples − 1 apple =

And she wrote with a shy smirk: 3 apples. Correct.

Then I wrote:

$4a - a =$

And she wrote: 3a. Correct.

Then I wrote:

4 of something − 1 of that thing =

And she wrote: 3 of that thing. Correct.

Then I wrote the original problem:

$4x - x =$

And she wrote: 3x. Correct.

Then I wrote:

$4x^2 - x^2$

And she wrote: $3x^2$. Correct.

Then I wrote:

$$5x^4 - 3x^4$$

And she paused, thought, and wrote $2x^4$. Correct!

The student began with not knowing $4x - x$. Rather than spend all the time necessary to explain what that individual problem means, which would have been fine, I sought to break down the concept to its most fundamental form and build her skills from there. Notice, this process did not require commentary, so I could have had tape over my mouth the whole time, as this chapter's title suggests. Finding the most basic concept and adding one wrinkle of complexity at a time allowed me to ramp up the difficulty in seamless increments. In fact, by the end of the short exchange, she knew how to solve problems even harder than $4x - x$! No wasted words got in the way of her and her thought process. It is always a win when your student can reach her own epiphanies without you having to say a word.

Body language

So much of what we study can be harnessed and illustrated through the use of our bodies, primarily with our face, arms, and hands. Communicators of American Sign Language literally embody this beautiful phenomenon daily. When the time is right, you can convey the exact message you wish by using your body as well. Using body language can be vastly more powerful than simply using words. We learn through kinesthetic movements; in fact, this is the original way humans learn during infancy, according to well-known developmental psychologist Jean Piaget (Blair-Broeker). Moving enhances learning in vastly more profound ways than words ever can. Our options are limitless; here are just some examples:

- using your hands as a balance scale
- modeling intersecting lines by crossing your fingers or forearms
- making your forearms parallel to demonstrate what parallel looks like
- lifting your flat hand to symbolize increase and lowering it to mean decrease
- bringing your hands together to demonstrate a combining motion and separating them to mean detaching
- pointing your finger in a variety of motions: up, down, left, right, back, forward, etc.
- counting on your fingers
- positioning your arm to portray 'vertical' and 'horizontal'
- gesturing to say "keep going" if your student needs to continue a process but does not realize it
- using the lateral swipe motion of your hand to symbolize "no more" or "stop here"
- smiling to suggest a variety of meanings, such as "that's right," "almost there," "not quite," etc. Choose your smile wisely.
- letting your eyes do the talking
- snapping your finger when your student has struck gold, which adds a nice emphasis to the moment

- giving a simple, sincere, one-person applause at a job well-done. This goes a long way.

As you demonstrate concepts through your body and become proficient at this strategy, invite your student to physically demonstrate when she has learned as well. What does vertical look like? What does a semicolon do to two clauses of a sentence? What happens to demand as price increases? Encourage your student to get in on the motions. The immediate uptick on learning is marvelous to witness.

Motion also keeps the body active and engaged, which is much more conducive for learning than being overly stiff or sedentary. Think of a group of kids at the playground. Tune in to their world, and you'll immediately see constant teaching and learning within the group. They say things like, "Look at this" before a demonstration or "Now let me try" to replicate an activity just seen. They are in perpetual motion, activating their bodies and their brains to fire on all cylinders. I don't recommend that you incorporate arbitrary motions during your One-on-One time. Motion must be meaningful. Simply look for opportunities to enrich your student's experience by learning through action. It is a fascinating art form, imprinting mental concepts on the mind via the body.

Chapter 8

THE FIVE S'S: TURNING THE INTANGIBLE INTO THE TANGIBLE

Think for a moment of anything you love about the beach. Swimming in the waves? The sun, sand, breeze, or open spaces? All would be wonderful answers. What if your answer went a little deeper, to special aspects of the beach we know are there but are not overtly visible? How about the feeling right when your feet first hit the sand, how you sink into it, the way it rubs and crunches down under the weight of your foot, the mix of whites, yellows, and browns when you look closely at the grains, or the sometimes unbearable heat on your skin? To say "the sand" is only referencing the tangible.

But to discuss how the sand shifts and feels or to tune into its colors and temperatures, is to reference the *in*tangible. The tangible is easy to describe, the intangible less so. But we must also identify the intangible in order to see the world more clearly, more comprehensively, and with a sharper awareness of our surroundings. The fascinating truth: shining a light on that which is intangible *makes* it tangible. Once an observation moves from the intangible to the tangible, it can be discussed, analyzed, improved upon, taught, and learned. This is my mission within education.

Here is my point—too much research and development in the field of education is based on that which is only tangible. Our leadership and our general culture have been obsessed with tangible, measureable metrics. Test scores, grades, and high-stakes standardized exams are hyper-tangible evaluations still deeply embedded within our system. The Common Core State Standards curriculum is a valiant attempt to pin down every necessary skill the students need to comprehend, but it is yet another display of our outright obsession with tangibility. And sadly, our teachers are assessed predominantly using tangible measures, mostly from student scores. The reason? It has been determined that we, as a society, need to have universal systems in place so that we can look at data and righteously say what is and what isn't, while sidestepping complexity and nuance. This student performs better than that student, this school over that school, county over county, state over state, country over country. I have a profound, fundamental disagreement with the way this system of tangibility runs. Sure, I'm fine with collecting data to improve programs. I'm fine with the tests and the grades as well, as I too give them in my classes. But unequivocally, tests and grades don't inspire. The second we believe that the tests and the grades are the point of it all, we lose.

During a school field trip, I had the good fortune to meet Elon Musk, co-founder of PayPal, founder of Tesla Motors, and CEO and chairman of SpaceX and SolarCity, respectively. In a candid setting, the students were given the chance to ask him questions. Eventually, one student asked, "What do you look for when it comes to hiring someone?" The room fell to silence as the students awaited his response. Would his answer align with everything they had been indoctrinated to believe regarding lower level education, that it is simply a tool to get into the right college, which will lead to an amazing job, which will provide financial security? I will never forget what he said.

He said that in addition to looking at a candidate's GPA, yet ranking far above this standard of assessment, his hiring committee at SpaceX looks for experience in engineering competitions. He spoke of the importance of performing at a high level, in imperfect conditions, under a time crunch, within a team of varying personalities. Which do you believe to be a more intangible construct: participation in an engineering competition or a GPA? The former is a high-speed collision of technical and social complexities. The latter is a number. The best part of the exchange was how intrigued the students were. They were downright relieved that someone so wildly successful advocated for an assessment tool that was unexpectedly non-academic. Though his words might have been suprising, they weren't shocking. The students fundamentally understood that successful engagement in an engineering competition organically reveals *far* more relevant data about a job candidate than an empty numerical snapshot in the form of a GPA.

Teachers feel the same about assessments of *them*. Across the board, in every state, the lion's share of teacher assessment comes from their students' test scores. But interestingly, ask parents what they want in their children's teachers and you get the more nuanced and the less tangible: integrity, fairness, gratitude for what they do, affability with kids, approachability, high socio-emotional IQ, etc. Of course, other tangible factors matter as well, such as a teacher's mastery of the subject, ability to impart material clearly, establishment of a good learning environment, organization skills, consistency with policies, commitment to regular communication, and professional demeanor, etc. But drill deeply enough into any tangible skill and we see that its complete mastery inevitably entails a journey into the intangible.

I am convinced that for whatever reason, our broader society is unready and afraid to pivot the conversation to the intangible when it comes to education. Fortunately, progress is evident, but it is still slow and not yet mainstream. For example, Hanover Research submitted a report on The Measures of Effective Teaching (MET) Project, funded by the Bill and Melinda Gates Foundation. The report examines the use of intuitive student surveys of teachers as part of the overall teacher evaluation. Questions from the MET Project thankfully cover intangible principles, such as "The Tripod Survey's Seven C's": caring, controlling, consolidating, captivating, clarifying, conferring, and challenging. The evaluation questions are grounded in these seven tenets. For example, one question asks, "After asking us questions, my teacher lets us think for a few seconds before we have to answer." This sounds a lot like our "non-response" approach from the previous chapter, does it not? **The prevailing reality is that good educators do the tangible things well. Great educators also do the intangible things well. One-on-One education is packed to the brim with intangible moments that we can identify, hone in on, and master.**

I have spent more than a decade meticulously tuning into the exact systems that inspire students to thrive. In my research journey for this book, I quickly confirmed that tangible directives dominate the landscape. To be clear, we need tangible directives. This book contains numerous tangible ideas about what to say and do. At the same time, within this book I have made considerable efforts to explain the intangible benefits of each tangible idea. For example, not speaking at times (tangible) taps into your student's inner voice (intangible). Synchronizing with what your student is currently going through (tangible) establishes trust and attunement (intangible). Or even the simple act of asking, "Are you sure?" (tangible) is meant to resurrect your student's dormant confidence and self-assuredness (intangible).

Now is the time to tie it all together. Up to now, I have outlined every tangible One-on-One strategy you'll need and offered each underlying intangible meaning. Now I will outline a One-on-One teaching/learning *system*. Naturally, true success at anything cannot thrive without a series of interrelated components simultaneously working in harmony. I am personally fascinated by the series of events that lead to a success story. What kind of communities groomed the young Abraham Lincoln with the resiliency to cope with his series of early political failures? What caliber of people surrounded the young John F. Kennedy and helped foster his massive intellect? And who amongst us now is quietly and systematically being groomed to be the next big thing? **Systems for success matter, and thus it is imperative to capture the essence of what makes intangible greatness, so as to recast it within concrete, tangible steps.**

The backbone of this system hit me at 5:30 a.m. one random morning. I dashed to my desk and poured it out on several pages of a legal pad. From that point on, I became highly aware of each component of this system, which I witnessed constantly at play all around me. It was like a magical pair of goggles had been placed over my eyes, enabling me to see the system in action everywhere I turned. I now hand the goggles to you.

This system is called "The Five S's," and it draws upon the metaphor of agriculture. The Five S's are Soil, Seeds, Soaking, Sun, and Surrender, in that order. As a disclaimer, to date I have not attempted much gardening in my personal life. Thus, I cannot tell you any specifics about how to grow a single plant. However, what strikes me is the uncanny number of intuitive parallels that exist between cultivating a plant and cultivating a student:

- Each component by itself is useless. Amazing soil is nothing without the right seeds. All bets are off without water, and so on. The same goes with education; each component within the system is useless without the others functioning properly alongside it.

- Growth takes time and patience, for both plants and students.
- Both "fields" gain their inspiration from making others bloom.
- The Journal of Alternative and Complementary Medicine cites the University of Arizona's Center for Frontier Medicine in Biofield Science's empirical proof that calm, serene energy nourishes plant life. The same goes for nourishing learning.
- At the end of it all, beyond mastering every tangible process we can to promote growth, we can only marvel that the most authentic growth sparks from that which is inherently intangible. The master gardeners and educators agree: that fleeting, indescribable instant of growth is borderline miraculous, leaving us in awe.

Soil—Laying the groundwork

You can't toss the world's best apple seeds into a sandbox and expect results. The same goes for One-on-One artistry: ground conditions matter first and foremost. A student can only thrive if he enjoys feelings of safety, trust, receptiveness, intentionality, and partnership. Any lack thereof creates major blockages. Let's briefly describe each:

Safety—In addition to basic physical and emotional safety, a student must not fear that he will be labeled "stupid" or anything else negative when first embarking on a One-on-One relationship. This mandate applies to all relevant parties in the periphery: parents, teachers, family members, friends, and community members. It is the One-on-One professional's job to protect and defend the student against anyone who strikes at his sense of safety whenever necessary. This includes even seemingly benign reactions like a parent sighing from across the room when she hears her child make a small mistake. Gently remind that parent of how vital it is that Michael be afforded the chance to make mistakes in safety.

Trust—Does the student believe that the One-on-One practitioner has the student's best interest at heart? Does the student have enough reason to go along with the practitioner's program, even if the student does not see the immediate point?

Receptiveness—Does the student feel seen and heard? Are her concerns immediately and thoroughly addressed? Is the One-on-One educator engaged in the moment and willing to approach their time together with positivity and aliveness?

Intentionality—Are the student's and the instructor's goals highly aligned? Is the pair working towards the same short-term and long-term results? Do they check in whenever necessary to re-align those goals?

Partnership—Is the balance of power intact? Meaning, is the student the most active participant in his learning, as opposed to the One-on-One instructor doing most of the work? Is the dynamic between them "bilaterally engaging," as in, both parties are intricately involved in the process, rather than the instructor blabbing away at the student one-directionally?

Notice that the "soil" phase is absolutely devoid of any technical expertise. Before any technical information can be exchanged, the soil conditions must be at least minimally met.

Of course, sometimes when One-on-One artists meet with students for the first time, after a brief synchronization, they need to jump right in to learning material. However, through the effective practice of One-on-One instruction, the soil will be cultivated along the way. For example, we know that trust cannot be firmly established in one or two meetings. However, once the student sees that the instructor approaches the craft from a place of caring and advocacy, trust will be kindled.

It is important to note is that most of the time, when people seek One-on-One support, they tend to omit this vital introductory "soil" stage. They say things like, "I need help in math. Who's good at math?" Obviously, the One-on-One educator must be an expert in his/her field, as will be discussed next in the "seeds" phase. But remember, technical expertise without properly enriched "soil" beneath it will only go so far, if anywhere. Case in point: thousands of math and science tutors worldwide are ready to personally assist students online in STEM (Science, Technology, Engineering, Math) fields, at affordable prices. Try a Google search of "STEM tutor (country)" to see. Why then do so many people who need help and can afford it, still go without it? Why do so many people still struggle with finding the *right* help? The reason has to do with these intangible soil-level factors, safety, trust, etc. Anyone can impart information here and there, which is fine. But not anyone can create and sustain a learning environment that surpasses the ordinary, opens the mind, and elevates learning to its maximum potential. Don't jump ahead to the content without cultivating the soil. Otherwise, you will merely be going through the learning motions, nothing more.

Seeds—Planting the right ideas in your student's mind

In this book, I have spent the least amount of time discussing exactly *what* to teach. This book dives into *how* to teach. Subjects are diverse, the complexity within subjects varies, and most importantly, each One-on-One relationship is different from the last. We all have our own teaching styles, which can be positively amplified by using the concepts, examples, and sample dialogues outlined in this book. Backed by all the strategies you've read here, this is the stage where you unleash your knowledge and expertise.

Take your student on a journey, starting at square one and building to square one hundred. Cross-reference, expand upon topics once your student shows some understanding, backtrack or jump around as necessary to check for loose bricks, diverge on a concept to build its case, then converge back to it using points you just made, have the student demonstrate understanding at every turn, ask "why?" and "are you sure?" regularly to check his conviction, use silence and body language teaching tools, and use every other artistic and technical skill that comes with effective teaching.

Fittingly, there is nothing more I can say regarding the "seed" level stage. The effectiveness of this stage has everything to do with your mastery of the subject. Wow them with your wisdom; they're ready for it now.

Soaking—Taking a budding mind from seedling to proliferation

You laid the groundwork at the "soil" level. You spread the "seeds" of your knowledge and taught some material. Now comes the stage that takes the most time and requires the most all-encompassing effort: "soaking." Think back to the budding seed. When it first cracks through its shell, it is so fragile. Any number of events, including minor ones, can impinge on the seedling's growth. The same goes for our students. At the initial moment of learning a concept, especially if it is very hard for them, the majority of their body's energy is intensely allocated towards their brains. Since their thinking systems are firing on full tilt, the rest of their body's systems are fragile, just like those of the seedling. Imagine the devastating effect of raising your voice or making a passive aggressive comment right at the microscopic instant when your student is on the verge of comprehending a point. He may first look at you in shock, because he is still highly vulnerable in that moment. But soon thereafter his walls will go up in resent, which is a deal-breaker to inspired learning.

I bring up the extremely negative example of what *not* to do in order to prove a point. What you do at this stage has extremely important ramifications. As your student takes small steps and improves, shower her with support and encouragement. Just as rain showers soak blooming fields, shower your student with support to let her "soak in" everything and bloom as well.

Try this field test, which is an exercise that anyone can do. It encapsulates a perfect One-on-One moment, and when done optimally, this activity beautifully offers many chances to "soak" your student in support. Here's the best part: *your student won't even realize you're doing it.*

This test is a basic numbers game. Challenge someone to add consecutive numbers sequentially. Once your participant understands the game, your sole job is to actively witness him/her navigate through it.

So ask your student to start with 1.

Then add 2, which makes 3.

Then add 3, which makes 6.

Then add 4, which makes 10.

Then add 5, which makes 15.

Then add 6, which makes 21.

Then add 7, which makes 28.

Then add 8, which makes 36.

Right around adding 8 or 9, this number game ramps up in difficulty. Notice how many times your student looks at you while thinking. Notice the number of cues he subconsciously seeks from you. Notice any insecurities hidden within that begin to come creeping out. "I'm not good at this stuff," she may say with self-deprecating laughter. "I'm not good under pressure," he may say, even though this is just a casual exercise. Notice the inward-outward dance generated. Into his mind he goes to think, and out he comes to you for feedback. I contend that a minority of people will either fly through this game with no problems or plod through the exercise meticulously, with zero historical baggage impeding them. The rest of us in the majority will accomplish the exercise with varying degrees of success, in varying degrees of stress, all resulting from our personal histories.

Your role while your student goes through the numbers is absolutely *crucial*. Hold her gaze when she looks to you. With positivity and sensitivity, tune into her and be ready to mirror back any feedback signals she needs. Once your student understands the game, try to communicate non-verbally as much as possible. Use universally understood facial cues, such as smiling, nodding, and blinking. These are concise cues that don't interrupt your student's flow. Affirmative facial expressions can communicate complex notions such as, "Bingo!", "Keep going," or "Yes, don't doubt yourself." Other facial expressions can communicate encouraging yet corrective statements, such as "Almost there," "Not quite," or "Go back." Throughout this process, you and your student are synergistically connected. You may notice that if you do your part consistently well by mirroring and silently supporting him through his journey, then the rest of the room will melt away and the two of you will be on a distant mental island together. This is where the magic occurs. I believe that the world's greatest and most fulfilling learning occurs in this elevated zone.

This is what soaking in support entails. Remember, support and encouragement are by no means equivalent to praise. You're the tuned-in spotter in the weight room or on the gymnastics floor. You're *not* the over-eager assistant coach on the team who attempts to win favor by tritely pouring praise on the players. Shower your student with support, soak them in encouragement during the throes of their learning, and simply observe as they sprout up from seed to sun.

Sun—Turn the heat up on their learning

Maimonides famously said, "Give a man a fish and you feed him for a day; teach a man to fish and you feed him for a lifetime." Our work as One-on-One artists is not done once our student learns a few tips and tricks. Our work involves the eternally more important task of igniting within him a curiosity to learn more and a burning desire to raise *his own* bar of excellence. Thus, the image of the sun is apt. The sun is hot, bright, and constant. It represents the degree of intensity with which we humans must strive in our lifetime pursuit of learning.

Once you have adequately "soaked" your student in support so that he has achieved some degree of ability, don't let up on him. In true sun-speak, hold his feet to the fire. You could say, "Yes, correct. Now that you see that, isn't it cool that the same rule applies for…" (Insert some other problem or condition). Or perhaps, "So you're saying that this rule works for *all* situations? What about ____ or ____?" (Insert alternative situations to challenge her). Condition her mind to explore, and as a team, "shine light" on any gaps either of you perceive along the journey.

A popular mantra in military circles, coined by Alexander Suvorov, encourages soldiers to "train hard, fight easy." In other words, work as hard as you can during the training phase; prepare and then over-prepare, so that the difficulty of the real battle will be relatively much less. When your student is ready, methodically condition her to *intensify* her learning. People are ready to put in serious work towards major goals; they just need the right conditions in place to feel motivated to do so. Up to now, you have been systematically creating those conditions. That is, you've worked to establish a fertile foundation at the "soil" level, you've offered your "seeds" of wisdom, and you've "soaked" her in constant support toward some success. Now like the sun, turn up the heat. Try saying,

"Ok it seems like you've understood the main principles well, nice work. So now I ask you: do you want to hit a home run on this test?"

Student nods in the affirmative.

"Great. If you do, then you need to make sure these concepts are ironclad solid in your mind. The way to do that is by getting lots of practice. I'm going to give you a good number of examples of each type of problem. After each, check the solutions page to see if what you have exactly matches. If it doesn't, try to find your mistakes. If you can't find your mistakes, let me know. Sounds good?"

"Yeah, I get this stuff now. It's actually not so bad once you understand."

"I feel the same way. And getting lots of practice is something all the greats do, so you'd be in good company. Practicing is the road to mastery, and this applies to anything we do in life. For this test, your goal is to anticipate everything that you'll see on it, so that when each type of problem appears, you'll be jumping with joy. Right now you say it's 'not bad.' Can we get you to a point where when you see a question on the test, you think, 'Yes! I love this type of problem! I *own* this test!' Better to proactively prepare that way than to only be reactive to whatever happens to be on the test."

"Totally."

You can even explain the "train hard, fight easy" mentality. Even if she is familiar with it already, let her experience the pride in knowing that she too can effectively train hard to achieve potentially high results. Model a "heat-seeking" behavior whenever applicable in this "sun" phase. This means that now you have the chance to exhibit the flame of *your* intellectual curiosity, possibly by referencing a story from your life about when you learned this material and what your personal challenges surrounding it were.

Now is also your chance to throw a series of progressively more perplexing hypotheticals at your student and make this a fun activity. One simple way to instantly establish a fun dynamic is to speak in third person about your student. Suppose he conquers a tough exercise and you say, "Boom! Ok, can he handle more? Let's see, shall we... what about *this*?!" and lay an even harder problem down. The key idea to bear in mind is that this style of high-octane intensity must be saved for the "sun" phase, no sooner. If you jump the gun and try to over-challenge too early, then your student will either despair at best or sour at worst. He may misunderstand your intentions too, thinking that you are punitively just making the work harder to prove something, such as how far behind he is, or that you're showing off, or you're just "nerding out," meaning taking personal joy in all the intricate details of a subject. "Nerding out" is great, but only when you can "warm up" to the subject and nerd out together.

Surrender—Sit back, enjoy, and let it happen

When I was a child growing up in Maryland, my father worked in a large building surrounded by open fields. His company thoughtfully provided each employee the option to use a 40-square-foot lot of its nearby land for personal gardening purposes. As he was already an avid amateur horticulturist, my dad took his "agri-bilities" to the next level. Every afternoon after work, he devotedly labored in that humid sun, tending to his assortment of plants. As the days turned to weeks and months, he began to bring home the fruits of his labor. Figuratively speaking that is, considering that he didn't plant fruits, only flowers and vegetables. At first, the rest of us in the family thought we'd be getting a few tomatoes and cucumbers every once in a while. But little did we realize, his crop yield soared to tremendous heights. Day after day, he brought home boxes packed with an assortment of tomatoes, cucumbers, spicy and mild peppers, and a variety of flowers and herbs. It was plainly too much for our family alone to consume. So he would seek out every neighbor or family member who could take some off our hands. Even still, we had excess.

He worked diligently in that space every day. He constantly learned from the process and improved, basing his education largely on the tacit feedback he got from the very crops he planted. What would anyone expect to happen in this situation? Of course his eventual return was to be astronomical. His persistence opened the floodgates, so there was nothing left to do but to be in a state of constant picking and eating. Nothing left to do but to surrender to this new reality of abundance. This story aligns with our students very well.

The "surrender" phase is unquestionably the best part of One-on-One practice. This is when the seeds of you and your student's efforts grow into a bountiful harvest. The harvest being that your student "gets it" and begins to soar. (Keep in mind, each student soars at relatively different levels.) What a sight to behold: she "gets" the concepts, she "gets" the value of working hard, she "gets" the feeling of pride from a job well done, and above all, she is fired up by intrinsic motivators over extrinsic rewards. Even though our job is mostly done, we still have a very important role during this stage.

"Surrender" means just that: back off and let the magic happen. Communicate to your student your awareness that he is exactly in the space he needs to be, and that you're so pleased to see such significant progress. But beyond this point, remember that less is more. Let your student's process unfold. Let him make one realization after the next at his own pace. Stay tuned in and provide small, corrective pointers along the way as necessary. *By no means should we make this phase about us.* Hijacking someone else's catharsis is one of the most selfish acts of social terrorism one can commit, in education or in general. Sit back and simply enjoy the show. As Tobias Fredberg writes in the *Harvard Business Review*, good leaders take the blame when it all goes wrong. But when it all goes right, good leaders *give away* all the credit. When you see your student flourish, pass all credit to her for stepping up. This is the service work we do; selflessness comes with the territory.

Imagine a movie-screening premiere with the movie's director in attendance, along with numerous audience members experiencing the film for the first time. After the lights have gone down and the movie has begun, you wouldn't see the director stand up in the darkened theater during a climactic sequence and belt out, "This one scene took me THREE full days to get right!" The creation phase of the movie was the director's time to incorporate all the magic he could. During the screening though, his work is done, and it is then up to the audience to "get it" or not. At peak moments when the audience may be moved to new heights, anything the director might say aloud could only ruin their experience. That's not to say that all dialogue with that director is unproductive. Afterwards, for example, the audience may want to arrange a Q&A session and personally engage with the director. Yet while the movie is ongoing and the viewers are on their respective journeys, we expect that the director in attendance should "surrender" to the moment and not say anything. Can we do this in education? Can we vigorously empower someone, and then immediately hand him back the reigns? Did we ever have the reigns in the first place?

Time and again I see educators talk when it's not helpful to do so. Maybe this has to do with some personal level of unease. Maybe this is ego-based. Either way, it takes a high level of maturity and security to let go of the controls and surrender at the right time. Choosing the right time to surrender is a nuanced art form applicable to a variety of life situations. In the middle of a romantic pursuit, a young man might erode his love interest's view of him by blabbing away unnecessarily. Or in legal procedures, some judges might favor a lawyer who knows when to remain silent and let the proceedings take place.

Lastly, we must not confuse "surrendering" with "giving up." Never give up on a student who is ready to receive help. "Surrender" means giving in to your student's natural process of growth and discovery, once you have helped regenerate it within her. Human beings are hard-wired to explore, experiment, learn, and ascend. Proof of this lies in small children. Have you known an otherwise healthy small child to be stagnant or lethargic? Not in the least. Their entire beings center on ceaselessly moving in and interacting with their environment. They examine, contemplate, and verify everything about the world as they come to discover it. At some point relatively early in life, largely due to our education system, society stripped them of that innate yearning for learning. High stakes rewards and punishments in our system supersede their instinctive, natural state of exploration. Help your students remember who they really are. And once you do, surrender, and simply stand out of their way.

Chapter 9

THE UNDERLYING TRUTH: TEACHING IS MORE ABOUT WHO YOU ARE THAN WHAT YOU DO

F lash back to a time when you gave someone a wrapped gift. As you handed it over, you might have noticed how both you and the receiver were already smiling. Then the time came to open the gift. Usually during a gift exchange, most people in the room focus on the person unwrapping the present. Some people, however, know to peek at the giver too. If your gift is in the process of being opened, and you are in the same room watching it happen, what do you feel at that precise moment? Excitement? Nervousness? Elation? It all depends on the gift, of course, but now suppose you know you are offering an incredible gift. A gift that took you time and energy to create, made in a way that only you can do. As the saying goes, "it has you written all over it." The receiver pulls apart the wrapping and peers in. Upon understanding the magnitude of what's inside, the receiver looks at you with joy and gratitude. Now what do you do? Instinctively, you mirror back the delight, expressing how happy you are that your gift is appreciated.

In a successful One-on-One dynamic, the teacher and student have an identical relationship to the giver and receiver of a gift. Isn't what you offer a gift? You possess something only you can uniquely give, and you present it to an interested receiver, with "you written all over it." My intention with this metaphor is to illustrate your role within this gift-giving paradigm. As your boxed gift is opened, which energy feels more appropriate to be in: half asleep or fully present? Of course you would want to harness the latter energy. You fundamentally understand the importance of meeting the receiver's excitement with an equal level of excitement. One-on-One education is exactly the same. All too often, educators fixate on content delivery and fail to realize the necessity of giving their students *energy*, much in the same way we automatically know to give energy to someone opening our gift. A common misconception is to think that giving energy debilitates the giver. Fortunately, though, this type of energy giving *invigorates* us. Don't we get a rush when someone opens and appreciates our gift? Doesn't it feel good to send a surge of warmth back to that person and share a moment together? Metaphysically, our bodies get a shot of serotonin, which is the feel-good body chemical associated with strong human connection. Giving energy is among the most elevated gifts we can offer anyone.

Let's explore this further. What are the most coveted, most valuable commodities we can offer others? Unquestionably, our time and energy. People who put time and energy toward their personal and professional endeavors deserve respect. If time and energy are among the top commodities we can give people, then we must conclude that this work requires us to truly *believe* that giving our time and energy is worth the effort. Time and energy given away without any overall belief in their cause is doomed to fail. Anyone who continuously siphons away her time and energy, without believing in the importance of doing so, ends up feeling immensely drained. This leads to eventual burnout and bitterness. I'm sure many of you reading this can testify to having had at least one teacher in your past who was burnt out or bitter. I certainly had a few such teachers. The chief culprit of burn out is the act of spiritlessly and endlessly doling out one's time and energy to no steadfast personal cause. We have an expression for those types of teachers, or for anyone who is burnt out. We describe them as being "over it." Their time and energy supplies have dried up.

This means that broad, long-term success in our work requires us to have a certain values system. That system's mission statement declares, "The only way I will engage in this work is with an all-encompassing, high level of personal investment. This is the way I would want others to teach me; thus, it must be the way I teach others." Going a bit further, we infer that the underlying power inherent in our work comes *not* from our technical expertise. Rather, it comes from *who we are*, as community members, citizens, and fellow human beings.

Think of the educators who taught you a lot or inspired you. Chances are that you respected them. What influenced your amount of respect? Surely, we acknowledge that the person had expertise and mastery in his/her field. But ask any student what factors earn their love and respect, and you will identify some common threads laced within their sentiments. You'll hear, "I could tell she really cared about us" or "He really wanted us to do well" or "We knew that she really wanted to be there." Embedded between the lines, the students are really saying, "This teacher cared enough to give us his all," or even more simply put, "She was good to all of us." Yes, students deeply appreciate someone who can eloquently impart knowledge. This is an essential facet of masterful instruction. Indeed, this book is full of ideas that will catapult you forward in your growth as a One-on-One artist. But what this book can*not* do is make you a better person. It can only serve to help you tap into that which is already good within you. Let it out, let it shine, for the macro-benefit of every student with whom you come in contact. The results of giving the gift that is you will echo throughout their lives.

While the One-on-One model has many unique challenges itself, the difference is that at the end of the day, the only elements that matter are you and your student. In contrast, the One-on-Many model of teaching bears numerous challenges, many of which are neither brought on by nor able to be solved by the teacher. Over-crowded classes, poor facilities, long-term checked out or abusive students, and administrative/

bureaucratic leapfrogging are just a few major examples of how modern day teachers are expected to perform under oftentimes difficult conditions. Unlike the One-on-Many arrangement, with One-on-One you have so much more direct influence. Students cannot hide amongst a sea of faces as they do in a crowded class, or stare off absentmindedly during lesson after lesson. Your student is personally accountable to you during every second of your shared time together.

My contention is that we feel most accountable to those whom we respect. Think for a moment: don't we all work harder and go above and beyond for the people we truly respect, such as certain teachers or supervisors on the job? As such, any *lack* of respect can dangerously undermine your student's desire to work, both for you and in general as time goes on. In his thought-provoking book, *Empowering Education: Critical Thinking for Social Change*, Ira Shor describes how disconnected students can go on an unannounced, unacknowledged "performance strike." When feeling alienated or disempowered by their teacher, they fail to perform at a high level as a form of subconscious rebellion. Which means, then, that the inverse of this phenomenon must be true. If a lack of respect for you leads to a performance strike, then an abundance of respect and admiration for you does wonders to motivate your student to excel. Their motivation draws strength from the very accountability they feel towards you.

A family once hired me to work with their teenage daughter for ACT prep. More than once, the student forgot about our appointments and was not home when I arrived. When that happened, mom did her due diligence to make her daughter accountable for the time and money that was still paid to me for those missed sessions. On one occasion, though, it was my turn. I forgot to mark the next appointment in my calendar, and I didn't show up for that scheduled lesson. Afterwards when I got the text message from the mother asking where I was, I blurted out, "Oh no!" I texted her back with an apology and offered some times to reschedule. Most importantly, I let her know that the session would not cost her anything. Mom ran with this idea. When I eventually went there (later that day it turned out), she asked her daughter to hand me the check sitting on the table, knowing I would politely refuse to take it. Interestingly, mom chose *not* to inform her daughter beforehand of my intention to decline the payment. Mom set up our interaction, so that her daughter would see me not accept it and subsequently witness firsthand what taking responsibility for one's actions meant. Needless to say, my student was very moved, realizing that I showed up just to work with her, without wanting a dime, fully happy to own my mistake. She also saw how I held myself to the same standards that her mother and I expected of her. It felt great to model this level of integrity, and naturally, the session was fantastic. Always seize the opportunity to demonstrate core values like accountability and integrity through small acts like this. These values not only strengthen your bond with your student, but also they help enhance your personal and professional reputation in the community. From every single angle, it's a winning move.

The gifts of time and energy lead to respect. But beyond respect, take a large step back with me and let's explore the successful application of time and energy to every walk of our lives. Oh, the relief we feel in making a customer service call when the person we reach gives us his undivided time and energy. Our political system and governance would be so much more effective if our elected leaders would invest real time and energy towards our common goals, as opposed to merely throwing around gimmicky, cop-out talking points that require minimal effort. Family life would dramatically improve if everyone in the home, including the kids, devoted their fair share of time and energy towards each other. And of course, the same idea applies to education.

Now let's make a final distinction between "time and energy" and "hard work." Over the years I have come into contact with hundreds of educators who work incredibly hard. I, too, work very hard. But time and energy are on a different plane than working hard is. For example, hard work for an educator may entail thorough preparation and execution. But an educator who gives time and energy is ever ready to be present to the hopes, fears, and dreams of his students. An administrator who works hard may be great at answering everyone's emails in a timely fashion. But a leader who gives time and energy *listens* to her team and is ceaselessly dedicated to implementing common sense guidelines that will benefit their lives. As we tune into this higher way of living, we come to appreciate how each investment of our time and energy is our chance to positively alter the course of society and make our personal mark on history. Just look into the eyes of an anxious student. You will see entire worlds of opportunities to instill goodness within him or her. Are you ready to approach this work from that consciousness, always aware of the influence you have to permanently affect lives?

Are you sure?

REFERENCES

Charles Blair-Broeker and Randal Ernst, *Thinking About Psychology: The Science of Mind and Behavior* (Worth Publishers, 2007), 265-267.

Peter Brown, Mark McDaniel and Henry Roediger III, *Make it Stick: The Science of Successful Learning* (Belknap Press, 2014), 46-47.

Katherine Creath and Gary Schwartz, "Measuring Effects of Music, Noise, and Healing Energy Using a Seed Germination Bioassay," *The Journal of Alternative and Complementary Medicine* 10.1 (Feb 2004), 113-122.

Carol Dweck, *Mindset: The New Psychology of Success* (Ballantine Books, 2007), 71-74.

Linnea Ehri, "Learning to Read Words: Theory, Findings, and Issues" *Scientific Studies of Reading* 9.2 (2005), 167-188.

Douglas Fisher and Nancy Frey, *Better Learning Through Structured Teaching: A Framework for the Gradual Responsibility* (Association for Supervision & Curriculum Development, 2013).

Tobias Fredberg, "Why Good Leaders Pass the Credit and Take the Blame." *hbr.org* (Harvard Business Publishing, Oct 2011).

Gayle Hilgendorff, "Why Do We Work So Hard?" *huffingtonpost.com*, AOL (November 8, 2013).

Alfie Kohn, "Five Reasons to Stop Saying 'Good Job!'" *alfiekohn.org* (September 2001).

Madeline Levine, *Teach Your Children Well: Why Values and Coping Skills Matter More Than Grades, Trophies, and "Fat Envelopes"* (Harper-Perennial, 2013), *xiv*.

"Media and Children." *aap.org.* (American Academy of Pediatrics, 2015).

Parker Palmer, *The Courage to Teach: Exploring the Inner Landscape of a Teacher's Life* (Jossey-Bass, 1997), 10-13.

Parker Palmer, *To Know as We Are Known: Education as a Spiritual Journey* (HarperOne, 1993), 70-71.

Ira Shor, *Empowering Education: Critical Teaching for Social Change* (University of Chicago Press, 1992), 20-21.

"Student Perception Surveys and Teacher Assessments." *dese.mo.gov.* (Hanover Research, Feb 2013).